SQUASH
HOW TO TRAIN, PLAY AND WIN

SQUASH
HOW TO TRAIN, PLAY AND WIN

VIN NAPIER

WINDWARD

Windward
An imprint owned by
W.H. Smith & Son Limited
Registered No 237811 England

Trading as WHS Distributors,
  St John's House,
  East Street,
  Leicester, LE1 6NE

This edition first published 1982

© Copyright Paul Hamlyn Pty Limited

Front cover photograph: Robin Eley-Jones

ISBN 0 7112 0246 X

Printed and bound by
The Burlington Press, (Cambridge) Ltd., Foxton, Cambridge CB2 6SW

FOREWORD

For years before we commenced playing squash Vin
Napier was building up a store of knowledge of
squash technique to help Australians reach the top.
His personal efforts to bring overseas professionals
to Australia were followed by close analysis of their
games and ultimately by clinics held throughout
Sydney to pass on his knowledge for the benefit of
young players. From these clinics Vin's first book
Squash Technique was derived and, with willing
players and coaches to assist, the road to success was
opened to those prepared to dedicate themselves to
the game.

Vin's fight and fund-raising to send the first and
sensationally successful Australian men's team
overseas and his fateful "discovery" of Heather
McKay and subsequent coaching of her to her first
world title made an impact on world squash as
decisive as it was surprising to almost everyone.

His continued efforts when others thought the
task hopeless were mainly responsible for the
formation of the International Squash Rackets
Federation (ISRF) and this was recognised by the
first official championships being allocated to
Australia in 1967. He was also one of a committee of
three responsible for the introduction of the
"Australian" ball which did so much to promote
stroke play.

Squash How to Train, Play and Win is based on
proven and updated technique. With his reputation
as a squash analyst it is not surprising that Vin has
introduced new ideas for teaching and studying
squash and the chapter on Training and Nutrition
is easily the most detailed and up-to-date treatment
ever accorded this important subject.

A former champion squash player, athlete,
administrator and analyst, Vin is ideally qualified to
point the way to another significant move forward in
coaching expertise. As he says, he has now done his
job and it is up to coaches and players to get the
results. We commend this book to you as a first class
production and a significant step forward in well
ordered squash instruction.

Dick Carter
Ken Hiscoe
Cam Nancarrow

PREFACE

Of all sports, I believe squash best combines the features of enjoyment and challenge.

At one extreme beginners immediately find both exercise and, unlike tennis, the thrill of the rally. At the other extreme top players demonstrate a very high standard of difficult technique, plus both physical and mental ability, developed through years of intensive practice and study. Between these two extremes are hundreds of thousands of players of all standards playing simply for the exercise and joy of the game, and perhaps for competition at their own level.

These features, together with the opportunity to play near home at any time during the week and in any weather, have undoubtedly led to the increasingly great popularity of squash both as an exercise and an exhilarating pastime.

Squash is believed to have originated in Harrow, England, around the middle of the nineteenth century. Students, unable to get into the sole rackets court, took their exercise hitting an india-rubber ball which squashed against the wall. This apparently suggested a smaller court and squashier ball and towards the end of the century almost every boarding school in England had a miniature rackets court on which a game with a racket similar to that used for rackets and a soft india-rubber ball was played. By adaptation of the rules of other games and modifications through trial and error over a long period, squash in its present form was finally developed.

It seems fairly certain that the development of squash technique commenced in Great Britain and the game is indebted to numerous British professionals who through the years built up technical skills.

A secondary development occurred when British servicemen and others carried the game to the Middle East, India and what is now Pakistan. In these countries a new cadre of professionals added their own particular stamp in varying ways to the British technique. In some cases outstanding proficiency was developed by professionals who started as ball boys for uncovered courts, had limited tutoring but unlimited time for practice, and developed their own technique.

The man who had the greatest influence on the standard of pre-war squash in Australia was a self-taught Australian, Percy Pearce. His early tutelage brought Gordon Watson to the position of third-ranked professional in the world in 1950.

The best of the post-war professionals of Egypt,

Pakistan and India were brought to Australia over a period of eight years (1949-57) but proved to be players rather than teachers at that time and it was left to Australians to analyse, question and interpret. A new technique based on the best of the varied existing techniques and on the Australians' own experience was finally developed and set the stage for Australia's domination of world amateur squash for more than a decade. Australians still hold the male and female world open titles in squash.

The names of Heather McKay, Geoff Hunt, Ken Hiscoe, Dick Carter, Cam Nancarrow, Kevin Shawcross and, in Australia's sensational first defeat of Great Britain, John Cheadle, Owen Parmenter, Ken Binns and Doug Stephenson, are known and respected in all competitive circles. Australia's leading contribution towards the formation of the International Squash Rackets Federation also played a part in Australia gaining increased world respect and a high position in the world squash community.

Squash How to Train, Play and Win is an exposition of modern thinking on squash technique developed in Australia. It is designed to take a player who has found enjoyment and physical fitness in squash through a complete course of instruction, making it possible for him to enter the top championship arena if he is good enough. Even if he has no such ambition it will certainly lift his game tremendously and put him securely above his present group of adversaries — and who doesn't enjoy that!

The book can be used for step-by-step instruction by coaches or, where no suitable coaches are available, by senior club members who have the good of the game and club juniors at heart. Some players became champions simply through teaching themselves from my previous book *Squash Technique*. Others did so through a mentor studying it and guiding their development. This new book is far better ordered and offers more comprehensive guidance for such a process.

I hope *Squash How to Train, Play and Win* will not only set the stage for the emergence of many new players who will emulate the great Australian champions of today but will also enable others to increase their pleasure and satisfaction in their own games.

Vin Napier

CONTENTS

INTRODUCTION   **9**
Competition squash — what to wear — the fundamentals of squash — glossary of squash terms

COURT MOVEMENT   **15**
Watch the ball — footwork and movement — pace — balance — final adjustment — exercises

STROKE PLAY   **27**
The basic stroke — the grip — the knees — the feet and body — a "grooved" action — the swing — limited horizontal swing — the full swing — racket head position — contact with the ball — position of the ball when hit — length and where to aim — the service — the volley — emergency volleying — the boast — the drop shot — the nick shot — the lob — eyes on the ball — the importance of practice — practice routines

THE BASIC GAME   **65**
The basic theory — pressure — the danger area — the service and return shot — the deep game — the short game — length — the lob — defensive retrieving from back corners — practice routine for controlling the game from the centre of the court

MATCH PLAY   **75**
A "pressurised" basic game — tight and tough — winners — the delayed shot — the mental approach — the first shots — attack with length — forecourt shots — down the wall — cross-court play — accuracy, position and observation — variation in pace — conservation of energy — balance — don't trail the racket head — patience and concentration — "pet" shots — other points to watch

POLISHING YOUR GAME   **91**
Experience — reading the game — when your basic shots are good — when you may be at fault — when the going is tough — tips for match play

TRAINING AND NUTRITION   **101**
Training — the basic theory — energy — interval training — types of training for squash — your training program — off-the-court interval training programs — male and female squash interval training programs — on-the-court training — nutrition — daily food requirements — the duration of work and the metabolic mixture — diet the week before an important event — the pre-game meal — the post-game meal — off-season diet — fluid intake

THE RULES   **119**
The official rules of the singles game of squash rackets — information supplementary to the rules — standard calls for match play — construction of a court — looking behind the rules

WORLD CHAMPIONS   **128**

INTRODUCTION

Good technique in squash is essential if you want to achieve maximum improvement and enjoyment in your game. To be proficient you must discipline yourself to continuously study and practice the basic fundamentals until they become instinctive.

Your aim in every squash match should be to:

(a) put sufficient pressure on your opponent to make him take a position deeper in the court and make him run from there as fast and as far as possible;

(b) keep the ball tight by always hitting shots least likely to be cut off by your opponent, i.e. always to the open court (which is so often down the side wall) to one of the four corners;

(c) make it difficult for your opponent to attack and continuously make him move more than you do yourself; and

(d) by sheer superior movement, sighting of the ball and stroke play gradually make your opponent struggle to get to the ball so you finally force a winner to the open court or a winner by wrong-footing him when he is racing to cover the open court.

You should seek to instil into your opponent the feeling that he is playing against a basic game which he cannot overcome by risky attempts at winners and against which he can not risk being out of position. In this way you put him under constant mental and physical pressure. Only when you have done this should you attempt either an open court winner or a wrong-footing shot which should be a winner because of the pressure applied on him to cover your basic game.

Points in a squash game are seldom won with one-shot brilliance. It is the lead-up to the final shot which is so necessary for consistent scoring.

To achieve your aim you must, by instinct and without intense mental or physical effort, be able to:

1. Position yourself well.
2. See the ball quickly.
3. Move with speed to take a position best suited to make your shot.
4. Make your shots consistently and accurately throughout a match, with maximum effect and minimum effort, from any point on the court and at any pace.
5. Recover quickly to the centre-court position which your opponent will have vacated in order to retrieve your shot.
6. Play through the whole of a long, sustained match at a constant high pitch of mental and physical condition.

The chapters in this book have been arranged in the most suitable order for you to progress from the basics to complicated match play. Strictly you should master correct court movement before learning stroke play, but in practice it is best to learn the limited horizontal swing (see page 33) to assist you when learning your court movements.

COMPETITION SQUASH

The controlling body of amateur squash (and open squash involving amateurs) is the International Squash Rackets Federation (ISRF). Its constituent members are the national amateur associations throughout the world. They in turn govern state, provincial and country associations which control the clubs within particular areas.

Professional associations operate in most countries where squash is played and there is also an International Squash Players Association to which most of the world's top professionals belong. Some countries also boast court owners associations which aim to standardise the control of public courts and to promote the game. Many of these associations control competitions under the aegis of an amateur association and, more importantly, make a special effort to help newcomers.

The strength and nature of clubs differ considerably throughout the world, from private exclusively squash clubs to squash clubs which are a portion of multi-purpose clubs and clubs which are exclusively for squash but which operate from rented courts.

To be eligible to play in most competitions you must belong to a club. To join, simply enquire at the nearest court or club or telephone your local association for advice on the steps to take.

When you get to the court ask a competent player, a professional or someone recommended by a club or court owner to give you the advice necessary to start playing. It is advisable to take along another newcomer who is of similar physical fitness and age as you so you can play with someone of similar standard until you feel ready to spread your wings.

WHAT TO WEAR

Having decided to play squash you will no doubt wish to dress and equip yourself satisfactorily.

For competition matches it has been customary to wear all white attire, including sandshoes. This still remains the only gear given absolute approval for amateur players by the ISRF. However member countries have been given the right to legislate if they so desire to allow clothing of a light pastel colour to be worn for events under their control. Many countries have approved this change.

In non-controlled match play there are few restrictions outside your own good taste. For optimum performance, however, it is essential that your clothing be neat, comfortable and well suited to the body heat developed in a hard match. Your sandshoes must be comfortable to avoid blistering. I prefer light shoes and two pairs of socks with a sprinkling of foot powder. You may find greater comfort in heavier shoes but this must be balanced against the faster movement attainable with light shoes.

A professional or experienced player can advise you in selecting a suitable racket. I prefer a racket weighing around 200g (7-7¼oz) and with about centre balance. It should be tightly strung.

THE FUNDAMENTALS OF SQUASH

Study as well as practice is essential to fast and enduring development of good squash players.

Heather McKay, over a period of 5-6 months, was coached assiduously from my previous book *Squash Technique* before going overseas to win her first world (then British) championship at the age of 20. During this coaching she reached the stage of reading the particular chapter involved in her training twice every day. She was the fastest learner of the game the world has ever known and she has never departed from the fundamentals she initially studied and adopted.

With the object of drawing the attention of all players to the necessity of giving first priority to learning the correct fundamentals of the game, seven highly qualified players—Dick Carter, John Cheadle, Ken Hiscoe, Geoff Hunt, Heather McKay, Cam Nancarrow and Owen Parmenter—and myself drew up a list of the fundamentals which we had found most lacking in juniors and most serious in retarding their development. By necessity the important matter of stroke play could not be covered, but the list is nevertheless vital:

1. Squash is a game of quick, smooth movement. There must be an instinctive fast first movement towards the ball every time your opponent hits it and a determination to get your racket to the ball at all costs. The first movement towards the ball (and from the ball back to the centre) must combine a sprinter's reaction to a starter's gun with a boxer's well-balanced footwork.
2. Turn with the hips and feet and in the second movement run facing a point a comfortable striking distance away from the ball. (See Court Movement to Hitting Position, page 17.)
3. Always watch the ball wherever it is and regain your position a metre behind the "T" before your opponent hits the ball.

4. While waiting for your opponent to hit his shot place your feet at 45 degrees to the wall on the side where the ball is and watch (full face) him hitting the ball.

5. Face the side wall (not the front wall) when hitting your shot. Feet must be either parallel with the side wall or the front foot nearer the side wall depending on your stride.

6. Always have your weight on your front foot when hitting the ball and hit it opposite your front foot. Fight to attain this position and balance.

7. You cannot succeed without most of your shots being pressure length shots. Use the full length of the court.

8. Subject to 7, think always of making your opponent play his return from one of the four corners of the court. Basically play to take him to the farthest corner (the open court—so often down the side wall) and never allow him to cut off your shot at the centre of the court.

9. Once you have your racket in forward motion don't try to hit with your body or shoulders.

10. Have the correct grip—the "V" formed by the thumb and forefinger should rest a little to the left of the centre of the top of the racket handle—for both backhand and forehand. Always carry and use your racket at approximate right angles to your forearm and hold it vertical in preparation for all shots.

Remember, also, that you can not become a squash champion unless you are basically a good athlete and prepared to dedicate yourself to proper physical and mental fitness. Hence it is axiomatic that training and nutrition become priorities from the moment you start to learn correct technique and continue to remain so until you eventually retire from competitive squash.

Finally, always observe and admit if you have fallen down on any fundamental techniques during a match and work on rectifying them. Never make silly excuses for mistakes or failures.

The Australian amateur squash team of 1966-71, with manager Vin Napier (extreme left). Unbeaten in six years of international competition, this team is probably the best ever in international squash. The players are (left to right): Ken Hiscoe, Dick Carter, Geoff Hunt and Cam Nancarrow.

GLOSSARY OF SQUASH TERMS

Amateur: In broad terms, one who does not play or teach squash for financial benefit.

American Squash: Rules much like the soft ball game but court is 30cm (12in) narrower, scoring in each game is first to 15 points with each rally counted irrespective of whether hand-in or hand-out won, ball is hard and very fast, and technique differs noticeably.

Appeal: A player's request to the referee for a let, a stroke (penalty) or a reversal of a marker's decision, or a complaint regarding miscellaneous matters of importance to fair play.

Associations: Bodies which control squash within the bounds of their constitution; mainly amateur organisations. Amateur Associations order of seniority: 1. International Squash Rackets Federation (ISRF); 2. ISRF national associations; 3. state, provincial, county or area associations; 4. associations governing portion of area covered by 3; 5. miscellaneous associations of particular interest to groups with specific common interests, e.g. City Houses Association, leagues clubs.

Professional associations generally operate within the boundaries of corresponding amateur associations and liaise with them. Members of professional associations are normally required to register with both amateur and professional associations.

The International Squash Players Association covers leading world professionals who qualify for membership by virtue of significant tournament success. Its main aim is to promote a professional circuit.

In some countries there are commercial associations, e.g. the Squash Court Owners Association of Australia, which seek to regulate and standardise the operations of their members, promote squash generally and, by delegation from the amateur associations, conduct tournaments embracing players not generally catered for by existing competitions.

Backhand Court: The area of the court left of centre, in which the player normally makes a backhand stroke.

Basic Game: A basic squash strategy of playing to the open court to make the opponent move as far and fast as possible.

Board: See Tin.

Boast: A stroke played to make the ball bounce off a side wall or the back wall before it hits the front wall.

Clothing: For amateur events players traditionally have been required to wear all white clothing. The ISRF or relevant national associations sometimes allow clothing of a light pastel colour to be worn for events under their control, as is the case in Australia. Clothing includes footwear.

Clubs: Players' organisations, varying in size from a few teams to hundreds of members. Properly governed by constitutions and affiliated with amateur associations, they are the basic units which provide competition, advice and social contact for squash players. They either own their own courts or rent them and details are available at the local association or nearest squash courts.

Court: The squash court is 9.7m (32ft) long, 6.4m (21ft) wide, 4.6m (15ft) high at the front wall and 2.16m (7ft) high at the back wall. The height on the side wall is defined by a straight line joining the line at the top of the back wall to the line at the top of the front wall. For complete details see Rules Appendix II, page 124.

Cross-court Shot: A shot hit direct to the front wall at an angle sufficient to make it finish on the side of the court opposite to the striker.

Cut Line: A line across the front wall, the top edge of which is 1.8m (6ft) above the floor, and extending the full width of the court. All services must hit the front wall above it.

Doubles: Played on a larger court than the singles court, but few such courts exist. The game requires a high degree of ability and co-operation for successful and enjoyable play. In practice, lack of double courts and danger from intensely competitive players playing doubles on singles courts has led to squash being virtually restricted to the singles game.

Down: The expression used to indicate that a ball has been struck against the tin.

Dress: See Clothing.

Drive Kill: A drive hit very hard from the fore-court down a little to above the tin so the ball rebounds quickly and dies before the opponent can return it.

Drop Shot, Drop Volley, Drop Boast: Shots hit softly with delicate stroking to just above the tin so the ball finishes close to the front wall.

Fair View: A player is considered to have a fair view of the ball if he can sight it adequately for the purpose of playing it.

Follow-through: The portion of a stroke which follows contact with the ball.

Forehand Court: The area of the court right of centre, in which the player normally makes a forehand stroke.

Game: A game is won by the first player to score nine points or, if hand-out elects at 8-all, the first player to score 10 points. It is the portion of a match corresponding with a set in tennis.

Game-ball: The call when hand-in needs only one point to win a game.

Grip: May refer to the manner in which the racket is held in the hand or the portion of the handle of the racket which is covered to assist in holding it.

Half-court Line: A line on the floor parallel to the side walls, dividing the back half of the court into equal parts.

Half-volley: A shot hit almost immediately after the ball has hit the floor.

Hand: The period from the time when a player becomes hand-in until he becomes hand-out.

Hand-in: The player who serves.

Hand-out: The player who receives service; also the expression used to indicate that Hand-in has become Hand-out.

Handicapping: Mainly for club or social games. Generally a player is given X points start, e.g. his initial score is X points or his opponent is placed on minus-X points, i.e. he must score X points before reaching the score of "love". An alternative or additional handicap can be that a player on each occasion remains hand-in until he loses two rallies (not necessarily consecutive).

ISRF: The International Squash Rackets Federation, which is the premier world body controlling squash.

Knock-up: Hitting the ball to one another or to oneself prior to a match; the total time allowed, jointly or separately, is five minutes.

Ladder: A continuing competition under which players are initially graded on a "ladder" but have rights of challenge against opponents above their grade to take their position. Normally the first or second challenge can be made to anyone above, but subsequent challenges can be made only to those one or two places higher.

Length Shot: In general parlance a shot which travels the exact length of the court to the end of its first bounce, but also may refer to any shot which forces the opponent to the furthermost point of the court to retrieve.

Let: A let constitutes annulment of the previous rally, which must then begin afresh.

Marker: The marker calls the score and the play — "fault", "foot fault", "out", or "not up" as appropriate. When no referee is appointed, the marker exercises all the powers of the referee. On appeal, a marker's decision may be changed by the referee.

Match: A match is a contest decided by the best of five games or, in certain competitions, the best of three games. Apart from a two-minute interval between the fourth and fifth games and a one-minute interval between other games, play in a match is continuous. Special exceptions are laid down in Rule 21 (see page 122) in respect of injury, bad light, etc.

Match-ball: The call when hand-in requires only one point to win the match.

Nick Shot: A shot which hits the front wall and then the junction of another wall and the floor on the full.

Not up: A term used to denote a ball which either is not hit prior to it bouncing on the floor twice or does not hit the front wall above the tin.

Open Court: That portion of the court which, by virtue of his position, the non-striker leaves most open to attack.

Out: A ball is out when it: touches the front, sides or back of the court above the area prepared for play; passes over any cross bars or other part of the roof of the court; or hits anything whatsoever outside the walls or their vertical extension. The lines delimiting the playing area, the lighting equipment and the roof are out.

Penalty: The term generally used to denote that the referee has awarded the rally to the opponent under Rule 17.

Point: A point is won by a player who is hand-in and who wins a stroke.

Professional: One who is registered by his country's national body of the ISRF (for example, the SRAA) to play or teach squash for financial benefit.

Quarter-court: One part of the back half of the court which has been divided into two equal parts by the half-court line.

Racket: The framework of the head must be of wood and the handle shaft of wood, cane, metal or glass fibre. The grip and foundation may be of any suitable material, generally leather or towelling, the latter being particularly suitable for those whose hands perspire greatly. The dimensions of the racket are shown in the Rules (see page 124). A racket weighing around 200g (7-7¼oz) and of approximate centre balance is recommended.

Rally: The complete sequence of strokes by both players from service to failure to make a good return.

Referee: The referee awards lets and strokes and makes decisions where called for by the Rules, and decides all appeals, including those against the marker's calls and decisions. The referee's decision is final. This authority is given in detail in Rule 24 (see page 123).

Return: A return is good if the ball, before it has bounced on the floor twice, is hit by the striker to the front wall above the tin, without touching the floor or any part of the striker's body or clothing, provided the ball is not hit twice or out. The hitting of the side wall by the ball, before or after hitting the front wall in no way invalidates an otherwise good return.

Scoring: Points can be scored only by hand-in. When hand-in wins a rally, he scores a point; when hand-out wins a rally he does not score a point but becomes hand-in. A game is won by the player who first wins nine points except when, on the score being called 8-all for the first time, hand-out informs hand-in before the next service that he has chosen to continue the game to 10 points. Matches are generally the best of five games but can be the best of three games.

Service: The Server must stand with one foot inside a service box, drop or throw the ball into the air and, before it hits the floor or a wall, hit it direct to the front wall to a point over the cut line and under the top-most boundary line of the wall. The ball must then return so that, unless volleyed, it falls to the floor in the back quarter of the court opposite to the service box from which it was delivered. When a player becomes hand-in he may elect to serve from either service box but, while he continues to be hand-in he must change the box after each rally.

The server is allowed two services unless his first service hits (a) the front wall on the tin, (b) any part of the court before it hits the front wall, (c) an area out of court, or (d) himself or anything he wears or carries before it has bounced on the floor or is lost under Rule 9 (b)

Refer to Rules 4-9 inclusive (see page 119) for full details concerning service.

Service Box: A square delimited area in each quarter-court. A service is a fault (foot fault) unless the server has one foot on the floor in a service box when he strikes the ball.

Shoes: Squash shoes must have white or light-coloured soles so as not to mark the court.

Short Line: A line on the floor parallel to, and 5.5m (18ft) from, the front wall and extending the full width of the court.

Stop: Expression used by a referee to stop play in a match.

Striker: The player whose turn it is to play the ball after it has struck the front wall.

Stroke: In general terminology, the act of playing a ball with the racket. In the rules, however, it is used to describe what is commonly called a rally, e.g. "A stroke is won by a player whose opponent fails to serve or make a good return in accordance with the Rules."

Tell-tale: See Tin.

The "T": Denotes the junction of the half-court line and the short line, where a "T" is formed.

Tin: The area from the floor to, and including, the red line 48cm (19in) above the floor on the front wall. Except for the service, the ball must be hit above it for the return to be good. Also known as the Board and sometimes as the Tell-tale.

Turning: A call made out of consideration for your opponent's safety when you turn right around to hit a ball from behind him.

World Championships: The name commonly given to the ISRF championships in amateur squash or to similar open championships approved by ISRF. Prior to the formation of the ISRF the British Amateur Championship was generally accepted as the World Championship.

COURT MOVEMENT

Every aspect of squash is important in making a champion, but no single aspect is as important as the subject of this chapter. Not only does it show you how to achieve the quick movement to the ball necessary for competitive success but, provided footwork and movement on the court are carried out as shown, it also enables you to approach the ball in the manner most conducive to correct positioning of your feet and body as you hit it. If you always aim at correct movement in practice you will maximise your use of correct stroke play.

Most players acknowledge the stroke play recommendations regarding the position and stance they should adopt (see page 31), and genuinely set out to do this, but due to their method of movement towards the ball they consistently find themselves in a position where it is easier to hit the ball with their feet and body wrongly placed than to correct their position to play the ball as it should be played.

The most sound procedure is to start with this chapter and not go any further until such time as you fully understand and unfailingly carry out the advice in all your court movements. If this is not done, it is my experience that when a player who moves incorrectly gets under pressure he tends to hit from an incorrect position as this appears to him to present the easiest and quickest solution. However, if you move correctly you should rarely find yourself in a bad position.

The most important aspects of good court movement are:

1. Watch the ball.
2. Your first movement must be with the footwork of a boxer (from good balance on both feet); your second movement as for a runner, facing the way you are moving.
3. Your first movement must be very fast every time; your second movement must maintain pace but ensure correct positioning for next shot. Always make the first movement before deciding against chasing an apparently impossible return.
4. In moving up and down the court keep well inside the area where you will take up your stance to hit your shot, i.e. move up and down the central area.
5. From a two-footed balance the first foot to move in the normal turn must be the front foot.
6. Turn with the hips and feet; the body as a whole must be relatively passive.
7. Be balanced in the two important positions:
   (a) when your opponent is hitting the ball; and
   (b) when you are hitting the ball.
   Pace will be achieved between these two positions. Don't rush into your shot.
8. Your correct position when your opponent is hitting the ball is normally a metre behind the "T", unless he is incapable of playing searching

length shots, in which case you may move forward towards the "T". Balance and correct position for making your shot are attained by making last-second adjustments with your feet and knees.

9. Always turn and watch the ball and your opponent if he is behind you. Your feet will be at an angle of 45 degrees to the side (and front) wall if he is level with or behind you.

10. Watch the ball wherever it goes and watch the swing of your opponent's racket, his foot placement, the head of his racket going through the ball, and the ball leaving his racket. Bend your knees when he swings into his shot and be ready to go.

11. Be balanced when you finish your shot to facilitate a quick recovery to the central position behind the "T".

12. When you have hit the ball, your eyes, head and shoulders should be turned to follow its flight as you return to the centre. Do not retreat from the front wall with your back to your opponent.

13. Don't over-run the ball or "plant" your feet too early. Last-second adjustment must be made to feet, knees, body and head to enable perfect stroking.

WATCH THE BALL

Many important principles are interlocked to produce good and fast movement, however the most vital of all is to always watch the ball like a hawk, wherever it goes and irrespective of whether the next shot will be hit by you or your opponent. Never take your eyes off it. Concentration on the ball throughout a match is essential.

FOOTWORK AND MOVEMENT

It is best to consider a squash player's method of moving towards the ball as two separate movements. Basically, the first movement is like that of a boxer and the second movement like that of a runner. The first movement is the more vital in determining your pace to the ball, while the second is more vital in ensuring correct positioning in hitting the ball.

To ensure pace you must be perfectly balanced on both feet and move quickly and fluently like a boxer immediately you have made your decision to move. When you have completed this first movement and are moving to hit the ball, you must maintain your pace and ensure that your body and shoulders are

facing the way you are moving. This procedure will always keep the ball in clear view and enable you to establish a correct position from which to make your shot.

In moving from the centre-court position to your hitting position the following principles must be adhered to:

1. Never run straight towards the point where the ball will be when it is to be struck.
2. Always move so that:
   (a) your last step (with your forward foot) is towards the forehand wall if you are hitting a forehand shot or towards the backhand wall if hitting a backhand shot; and
   (b) if possible, you are about 1.5 metres (4½ft) from the ball if you are hitting a shot with a full swing, or somewhat closer if you are in the forecourt and wish to leave your options open as to short or long shots to either near-side or cross-court.
3. Your body must face the side wall when making your shot.

The diagram opposite indicates tracks for court movement from the centre to hitting positions.

When you are waiting to see which way your opponent is going to hit the ball you must have your weight evenly distributed on both feet and be on your toes. When you are on your toes it is easy to go forward or turn and go backwards. If you are on your heels it is virtually impossible to move forward quickly.

The position of your feet when you are waiting for your opponent to strike the ball will depend on where he is. Only when your opponent is hitting from near the front wall is there any reason for having your feet and body anywhere near facing the front wall. The extent to which you vary from this position will be determined by how far back in the court he is hitting the ball from. For instance, if he is on the backhand side you should gradually bring your left foot back as his position progresses away from the front wall. When he is alongside or behind you your feet should make an angle of 45 degrees to the front wall with your left foot at the back. The opposite would apply on the forehand side.

If your opponent is close to the front wall it is advisable to position your feet so that your movement forward is not dependent on having them exactly parallel to the front wall because every little bit of leverage helps in the first movement. Turn them a little so that the foot on the side where the opponent is will be a little behind the other.

If your opponent is hitting the ball from the back of the court you will have positioned your feet at an angle of 45 degrees to the front wall. You must turn

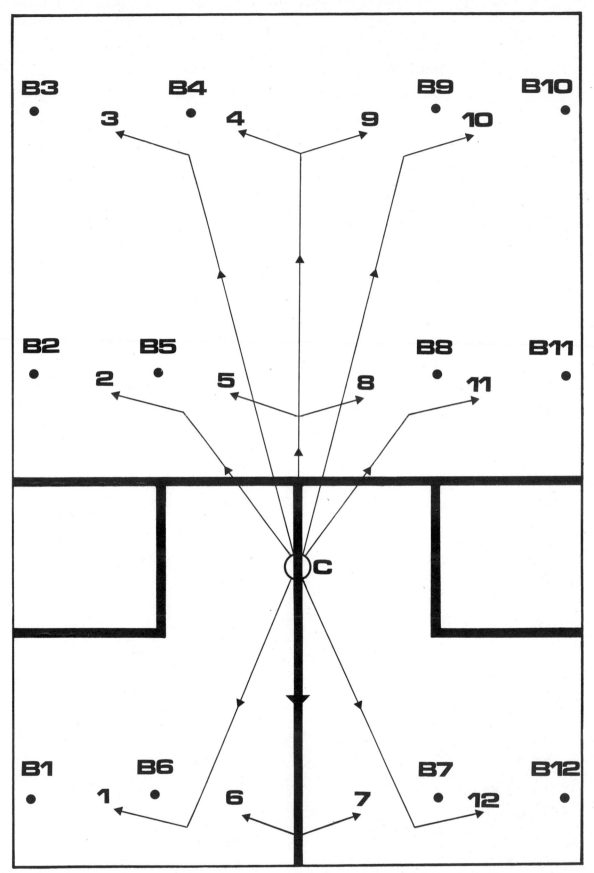

Court Movement to Hitting Position: These are the ideal training paths from centre-court position C to hitting positions 1, 2, 3 ... 12 to hit balls at B1, B2, B3 ... B12 respectively. The last step carries weight on to the forward foot for stroking (right foot on backhand or left foot on forehand).

The non-striker (above) is ready to move quickly to her shot. Her feet are at 45 degrees to the side wall and she is watching the striker, holding her racket head up. The non-striker (above left) stands with her feet parallel to the front wall, watching it instead of the striker. She does not see the ball quickly enough and does not have either her racket or her feet well placed to play her shot early and from a good position.

The striker (above) takes a path up the centre and across to a comfortable distance from the ball so that he is ideally positioned to play any shot accurately at any pace. The striker (above left) takes a direct path to the ball, putting himself in a bad position for stroke-making. This causes cramped action, limited choice of shots and an unconscious lifting of the head which in itself ruins his shot.

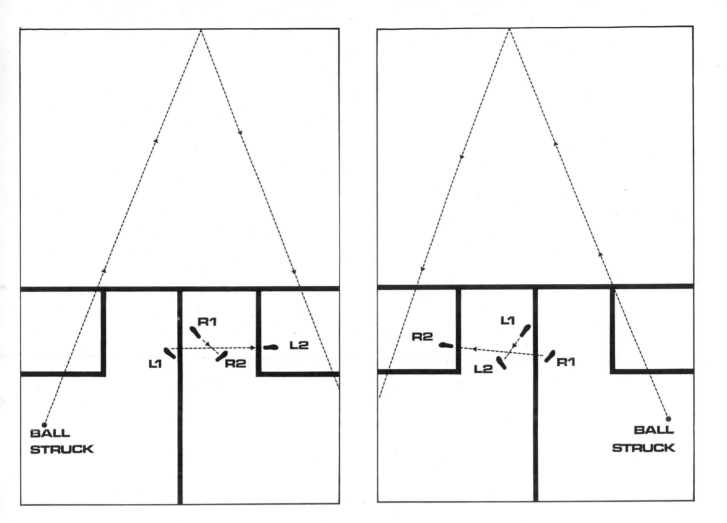

Movement to intercept a ball hit across court from deep in the backhand court (above left) or forehand court (above right): While watching the striker hitting the ball, the non-striker's left and right feet should be at L1 and R1 respectively. The first movement is to turn the hips clockwise (above left) or anticlockwise (above right) and step sideways so that: (above left) the right foot is at R2 and facing at 90 degrees to its original position, or (above right) the left foot is at L2 and facing at 90 degrees to its original position. Continuing this hip (and by now, body) movement, the left foot is then placed at L2 (above left) or the right foot at R2 (above right) to intercept the ball.

your head and shoulders so that you have a full face view of the ball being played. This position gives you the opportunity to see the stroke being played (i.e. direction of swing, racket through ball) and the ball movement both before and after it is struck. This, together with the 45-degree foot position, facilitates quick movement to three corners of the court, the only difficult movement being to turn around to intercept or chase a hard cross-court drive aimed to finish at the corner immediately behind you.

It is, of course, essential to turn around before taking this cross-court shot. This involves the most difficult footwork and movement on a squash court and pinpoints the need to always move the front foot first and turn with the hips and feet leading the body.

If properly performed the first movement of the hips and feet will automatically turn the body to face the front wall and without conscious effort the

second movement will follow through so that you face the wall towards which the ball is travelling. If you try to consciously turn your body you will seriously slow the pace with which you are able to turn. Think in terms of hip and foot movement and you will get to the ball quickly and easily.

Once you have learned to turn with the hips and feet leading it will become a natural part of your movement and not require conscious thought.

These movements are shown in the diagrams above.

The size of the steps in these movements will depend on the individual. Many players, due to their height, can cover most shots with two steps. But you may find it best to practise short dancing steps initially, then when the habit has been firmly established adjust the steps to conform more to your usual movement. Shorter steps can be faster and make turning easier. Physique and natural move-

NO

YES

After making a shot near the front wall the striker (above) turns and moves back with a good view of both the ball and her opponent, and good balance for a quick change of direction. The striker (above left) retreats backwards with bad balance and no view of either the ball or her opponent.

ments differ and cannot be ignored, but the movement of the front foot first and the turning of the hips and feet while keeping the body as a whole passive must be the basis of the first movement.

This habit of always moving the hips and front foot first is difficult to learn while playing squash as you will be continually distracted by the many other considerations of an actual game. Practise it away from the court by "shadow-sparring", simulating movements during a game. You must do this every day and it will probably take several months to perfect.

Your footwork and court movement after hitting the ball must ensure that your eyes, and therefore your head and shoulders, are turned to maintain a good view of the ball. Leading with the hips and feet, always turn towards the side of the court to which you have hit the ball and regain your position in the centre of the court while still watching the ball carefully. This ensures that if you have made your shot from up front of the court you can move

smoothly with full sight of both the ball and your opponent rather than retreat awkwardly with your back to him and the ball as so many players do. Your knees will be correctly positioned to quickly alter your direction if necessary and to take up your stance at the centre to watch and wait for the next shot to be made.

The best way to learn how to watch the ball and move correctly and quickly on the court is to play daily with a coach who continually stops the game when you are in error and coaches you in the principles expounded above. However, as this is seldom possible the next best method is for two learners to play against one another without using a ball (see Exercise 2, page 25) and when that has been mastered, to train on Phantom Squash (Exercise 3). Exercise 2 teaches you to watch an opponent's racket and get the earliest possible indication of where the shot might go, while Exercise 3 helps you to co-ordinate all the basic principles you have learned from this chapter.

PACE

Pace is measured from the moment your opponent hits the ball until the moment you are balanced and ready to hit the ball yourself. If you concentrate on pace during the period between these two points of time you will speed up the game and make your opponent move quickly, without losing your accuracy by rushing into your shot.

It is not possible to attain optimum pace unless you are poised in centre court ready to move when your opponent hits his shot. So, the instant you complete your own shot you must move quickly to centre-court while watching the ball and your opponent.

One of the greatest weaknesses of inexperienced players is that they do not realise how very important it is to turn and watch the ball, and their opponent playing it, when it goes behind them. Many players with quick reflexes waste their advantage by watching the front wall or half-watching the action over their shoulders. In doing so they are simply conceding a start to opponents who see earlier where the ball is going.

When you hit a ball that takes your opponent to the back of the court you must turn and watch firstly, the ball, and secondly, the action of your opponent when hitting it—the direction of his racket swing, his foot placement, the head of his racket going through the ball, and the ball leaving his racket. Foot placement and the direction of the swing often give you an early clue about his intention, but the head of the racket going through the ball and the ball leaving the racket are the vital things to watch in every stroke.

If you stand with your back to your opponent you do not know what he is going to do and if he is good enough he can hit a winner. It is absolutely essential that you turn, get your feet in a balanced position and watch the ball being hit so that you move quickly instead of being left flat-footed. This is the secret of pace on the court. Being a fast runner doesn't make you a fast squash player. It is a matter of split-second movement off the mark from the moment it is possible to know where your opponent is going to hit the ball. So, gain time by watching him make his shot and being ready to go.

If pace is applied immediately, the second movement and the preparation to hit the shot can be less hurried, resulting in improved stroking of the ball. Never take the view that pace is not necessary until the second movement. A quick first movement brings almost all shots within reach. Never consider giving up in even the most impossible position until you have made your first movement and then assessed the situation.

Champions are usually said to have exceptional "anticipation". They appear to know where the ball is going and be waiting for it. Generally this quality arises directly from following and practising the advice given above. However there are also special circumstances that merit risk-taking.

Firstly, a champion knows the strengths and weaknesses of his opponent and, in particular, his limitations in making a return when pressured into certain defensive positions. Very often, having made an attacking shot, he knows almost without doubt where his opponent must hit his return and, while still watching him closely, makes a preliminary move in that direction before the ball is hit. This is a good ploy, but it takes years of experience to master and the danger of an unexpected shot is always present. Hence he must watch the stroke being played no matter how confident he is. The counter to this "anticipation" is improved stroke play and a delayed shot which catches the early mover out of position.

Secondly, if the standard of the opponent is such that assumptions as to the stroke that will be played are dangerous, the true champion gains advantage soundly by: closely studying his opponent's usual stroke play and positioning (feet in particular); making lightning assessment in play from his opponent's actual positioning, forward swing and direction of face of racket through ball; and getting his final confirmation by the flight of the ball after being struck.

Anticipation through observation by the non-striker and concealment of intentions through perfect positioning and stroke play by the striker represent a little understood but most important battle in championship squash. The compromise usually adopted when players are evenly matched is that the non-striker from time to time backs his judgement by making an early assessment and commencing a slight move in the centre area. If his assessment is confirmed by the flight of the ball as it leaves the opponent's racket he is able to make a "moving start" rather than one from an absolutely stationary position. To do this safely, however, you must heed the following points:

1. Never move more than about a metre before confirmation.
2. Keep in an evenly balanced position on both feet while awaiting confirmation.
3. Don't guess. Only make a preliminary move if you can observe and assess with confidence.
4. If you and your opponent are well matched it seldom pays to make a risky preliminary move as this may be what he is waiting for. Save it for when you have him stretching and his options are limited.

In the heat of a championship rally, former champions Dick Carter (left) and Ken Hiscoe (right) demonstrate the value of years of practising correct movement. Hiscoe is perfectly balanced to do any shot he wishes. His weight is firmly on the front foot and his eyes are concentrating on the ball, which he is going to meet opposite or in front of his front foot. Carter is ready to move at the earliest possible moment. His feet are at 45 degrees to the side wall, his knees are well bent, the racket head is on the way up to the vertical position and his eyes are on Hiscoe's racket.

5. Skill comes only from long experience of continuously observing and assessing.

Note: A further important component influencing the overall pace of the game is the interception of the ball as early as possible and the striking of it in front of your front foot. This is discussed in detail under Position of the Ball when Hit (see page 41).

BALANCE

The two most important positions in squash—when you are hitting the ball and when your opponent is hitting the ball—require perfect balance.

When you are hitting the ball, you must be perfectly balanced so you can hit it in whatever manner and direction you wish. Your feet and body must be in the correct position and you must not be running or in any way rushing into your stroke. You must arrive at the point where you wish to strike the ball with sufficient time to get adjusted and stroke it accurately.

In making your stroke, the position of the ball in relation to the front foot is vital (see page 41). If the ball moves unexpectedly, move your feet and adjust your knees to maintain this relationship—don't hit it from a bad position.

When your opponent is hitting the ball you must pay just as much attention to balance and placement of your feet as you do when you are hitting the ball, and also position yourself so you can cover any shot he may hit.

If you have played your opponent away from the centre of the court your correct position is normally behind the "T".

Where there is pressure from length shots your position would normally be a metre (about 3ft) behind the "T". If your opponent is not a strong hitter you may move forward, closer to the "T", but this will depend entirely on circumstances and the type of game being played. In most cases you should take up the former position. From this position you have no fear of being hit and can watch the ball and your opponent making his shot, and ultimately command the game. Take up this position whenever you can and never fail to turn and watch if your opponent is behind you. (You will see later, in the chapter covering the basic game, that the ideal strategy is to make your opponent play his shot from one of the four corners while you watch him from the centre-court.)

Having taken up the best position available and balanced yourself evenly on both feet, watch the ball and your opponent striking it and you will be ready for any shot he may play. As he bends his knees to play his shot, bend your knees also so that you are ready to go.

As soon as you know where he is going to hit the ball, move quickly and correctly to the point where you are going to hit the ball, get into your striking position, gain perfect balance, and hit it firmly.

It is also important that you are suitably balanced to move quickly back to the centre after hitting the ball. Do not, on any account, start to move away from the ball before you have finished hitting it. "Stay on the ball" until your racket has finished hitting through it, otherwise you will lose accuracy and power. However, do not wait until the full follow-through is completed before moving. Merely stay long enough to ensure that the ball is struck correctly.

You must practice maintaining your balance and moving quickly from the moment the ball leaves your racket for two reasons:

(a) you must regain the centre of the court or best available position as soon as possible so that you are balanced and watching your opponent hit his next shot; and

(b) you must get out of the striker's way and do all you can to avoid interfering with or crowding him in getting to the ball.

In moving away from your stroke you must always consider the position of the striker and where he will strike the ball. He must be regarded as having right-of-way and you must do everything possible to allow him to get to the ball with a minimum of interference. If you stand still or move slowly, any interference will result in a let, or possibly a penalty, against you. If you do the best that can be done by a player in your position to avoid interfering with the striker, you are meeting the requirements of the rules.

If you correctly position yourself, correctly interpret your opponent's shot and quickly sight the ball after it has been hit, you should always be able to take advantage of the advice of this chapter and play

shots which will place your opponent under pressure.

FINAL ADJUSTMENT

Correct movement to the ball enables you to make your stroke correctly, but no matter how well you have done this it is the final adjustment which makes or breaks a perfect stroke.

When you see the ball leave your opponent's racket you must, from constant practice, be able to immediately assess where you will meet it and make your stroke. You must school yourself to near perfection in this assessment and immediately move in a manner designed to bring you to the hitting area, with your body and feet prepared to assume the correct hitting position and early enough to take the last step or make a last adjustment when you are able to pinpoint the exact point of contact.

Do not over-run the ball or "plant" your feet firmly before you are sure of the exact point of contact. So many people with seconds to spare "plant" their feet first and then take the ball wherever it comes, sometimes in the most unbelievable places.

You must remain mobile until you are sure of the exact point of contact, and you should generally have almost completed your backswing when your front foot (which is the last put down or to which weight is applied) is placed in its hitting position. No matter how much time you have or how apparently definite the point of contact may be, your feet, knees, body and head must have a final adjustment.

EXERCISES

To be effective, all court movements must be made smoothly and automatically. The following exercises have been designed to achieve this and you should practise them constantly.

Exercise 1

This exercise simulates a shot in which you are standing with your feet at 45 degrees to the side wall and watching a ball being hit from one back corner, then turning to retrieve it from the other. Treat it as similar to practising athletic starts for a short sprint.

1. Stand with knees bent, feet level and toes pointing forward, with your eyes watching an object on your immediate left.

2. Turn your hips and simultaneously step sideways with your right foot so that it points 90 degrees to the right of its original direction.

Australian Heather McKay, one of the world's greatest sports stars of all time. In 16 consecutive years as women's world squash champion, she has never lost a match. At world championship tournaments she has only ever dropped two games and on one occasion won the semi-final and final without losing a single point.

3. Continue the hip movement and bring the left foot around and over the right foot and run 5 metres (about 5 yds) in the direction opposite to that which you originally faced.

Complete the exercise in the minimum possible time without making any effort whatsoever to turn your body and shoulders. Aim to use your hips and feet alone and let your body follow automatically. Then repeat the sequence in reverse, i.e. commence by looking to the right, step sideways with your left foot and point it 90 degrees to the left, and cross over with your right foot.

Exercise 2

You'll need another player for this exercise in which you play a complete game without a ball but with the assumption that serves, length shots and short shots finish near the appropriate corners. Each of you must move correctly in every technical respect (in particular, follow the Court Movement to Hitting Position, page 17) and must determine where your opponent hits the imaginary ball by watching his position, swing and follow-through. If you incorrectly assess the corner to which the imaginary ball is hit, you lose the rally. All shots must be hit with a correct swing (see page 33) and as though a ball were actually being struck.

Exercise 3

This exercise, commonly known as Phantom Squash, simulates a match. It requires two people, an instructor and a player. The instructor directs the play and the player moves—technically correctly and at full speed—as directed, plays his imaginary shot and recovers quickly to the centre ready for the next direction. This procedure co-ordinates the basic features of court movement and helps build up stamina. The rules are:

1. The instructor stands in one of the back corners, moves across to the other back corner and returns according to how he directs play.
2. He raises his forefinger clearly in the view of the player as a sign that he has commenced to make his stroke.
3. He follows up by pointing to the corner to which he has hit the ball and the player must move at full speed to that corner and make his stroke.
4. The player must always play his imaginary shot down the side wall (full length).
5. The player must turn and watch the instructor while returning at maximum pace to the centre position so that he can assume a position of balance when the instructor indicates he is about to make his next stroke.
6. The instructor follows a tactical game of both moving the player to the open court and of wrong footing him fairly consistently to test his sighting, movement and stamina.
7. Rallies and spells between rallies should be of average match duration, say 27-second rallies and 3-second spells.
8. The aim should be to make the player always move at maximum pace. Occasional movement up the court by the instructor to simulate a volley is advisable to bustle the player.

Correct footwork, movement, pace and balance must be followed throughout this exercise and you should also use the full swing as soon as you have learned how to do it (see page 36). The Court Movement to Hitting Position diagram (page 17) must be followed.

Exercise 4

You must regularly do exercises to sharpen your reflexes and increase your potential speed in the first movement. Suitable exercises include athletics sprint training in running shoes, concentrating on starts; and skipping, moving the feet about with good balance—27 seconds skipping, 3 seconds interval, and repeat.

STROKE PLAY

Squash stroke play is a sophisticated and highly technical subject.

The squash racket is light—around 200 grams (7-7¼oz). The ball is of low pressure—it squashes on impact—and is generally taken on the fall. You therefore cannot take much pace from your opponent's shot but must hit the ball with great racket head speed, as in golf, to produce pace in your shot. As the ball has a low bounce you must bend your knees and get down to see and meet it at precisely the right point along its line of flight to ensure accuracy.

It is essential to play the ball out of an opponent's reach, and as the court is small you must be extremely accurate to prevent the ball from rebounding from the side or back walls and facilitating his shot.

Fast movement to and from the ball is essential and requires expert footwork and positioning to enable you to hit the ball in almost any direction (not merely straight ahead) and to disguise your intentions so your opponent has minimum time in which to prepare his shots.

The basic principles of stroke play are:

1. Use the same grip for backhand and forehand shots.
2. Face the side wall with your front foot nearest the wall when hitting your shot.
3. Bend your knees and get down to the ball for balance and accuracy.
4. Learn and perfect the use of a large arc of the hand and racket.
5. Hold the racket vertical at the start of your swing and keep it close to 90 degrees to your forearm throughout the swing.
6. Move the racket head in a continuous movement in a vertical plane in the backswing, then in a horizontal plane to hit the ball.
7. Make one continuous swing but first learn to use the limited horizontal swing at full pressure. Young children should use only this limited swing.
8. In the full swing the first movement in backswing is by the hip and elbow and in the forward movement by the elbow.
9. Wind up in backswing with the racket head trailing the elbow and then going over it and back behind the body. Concentrate from this point on getting the racket head to the ball ahead of the hand in a horizontal plane using full pressure of the forearm, wrist and hand.
10. Once forward movement is commenced hit only with your arm—keep your body out.
11. Generally hit the ball at knee height. Reach out wide to hit it opposite or in front of the front foot with your weight predominantly on that foot. (On the forehand hit a little in front for a down-the-wall shot and 30cm (12in) for cross-court. On backhand hit 40cm (15in) in front for down-the-wall and 60cm (24in) for cross-court.
12. Make a flat follow-through with the racket opening and finishing towards vertical over the left shoulder (forehand) or right shoulder (backhand).
13. Use the same backswing and foot placement no matter where you are aiming your shot.
14. For a cross-court shot, hit the ball closer to your feet and further forward.

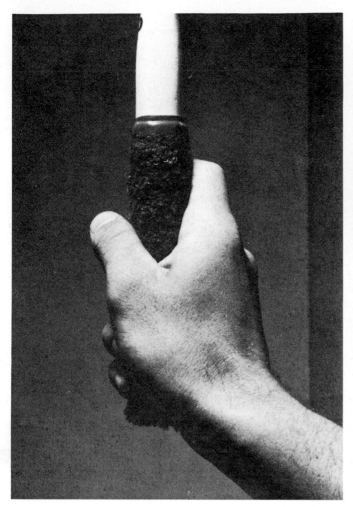
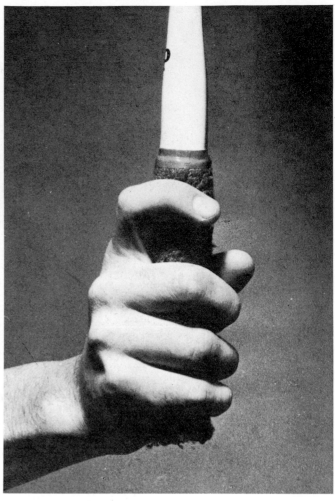

The same grip must be used for all shots. The "V" formed by the thumb and forefinger (above left) is a little to the left of centre on top of the racket grip. The fingers are spread comfortably (above right), with the "feel" in the fingers rather than in the palm of the hand.

THE GRIP

15. The ball is usually hit on the fall. It is not necessary to hit it on the rise except to maintain court position.
16. Vary the height that your shots hit the front wall to attain good length from all positions.
17. Service is a mechanical shot and must hit the side wall.
18. Use a firm action for volleys.
19. Boast with an open racket. The further forward you are in the court, the more open your racket.
20. A drop shot must be made with a simulated fast shot backswing and be sliced.
21. A nick shot should not be used when any return from it cannot be covered.
22. Hit a drive kill well out in front.
23. Lob high and diagonally.
24. Keep your eye on the ball.
25. Practice stroke-making on your own or with a friend.

Practice routines are given at the end of this chapter.

THE BASIC STROKE

The predominant stroke in squash is a length shot hit from between the short line and the back wall. It must have sufficient pace and accuracy to place pressure on your opponent, therefore the racket head speed at contact must be high and the path of the racket head must be horizontal (or near to it) well before contact and during the immediate follow-through.

To achieve these two features smoothly and with a minimum of effort you must have a large arc to your swing and a horizontal line of approach to the ball. This basic stroke should be the foundation of your stroke play and all other strokes should be derived from it with a minimum of variation, to achieve both efficient stroke play and maximum deception.

Of course, many shots have to be made hurriedly (for example, at the front of the court or on a volley). In such circumstances it is best to keep the stroke unchanged in its basic features and to achieve

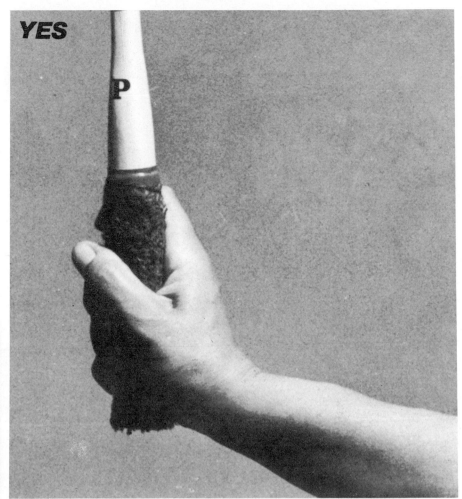

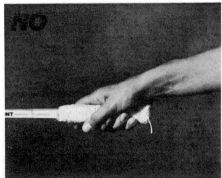

For correct stroking, the forearm must be close to 90 degrees to the racket (above). If the wrist and racket head are dropped (above left) stroking will become inaccurate.

quicker stroking by reducing the arc. Pressure of match play tends to cause many players to reduce the arc on all strokes, but for optimum power and accuracy, make every effort to maintain the large arc by starting the swing early when under pressure.

After a period of protracted match play it is always advisable to go back and again practise using a large arc as the basic stroke.

You should always hold your racket at approximate right angles (90 degrees) to your forearm. In practice the actual angles will probably vary between 100 and 120 degrees, but only by aiming at 90 degrees can you achieve consistent stroking.

THE GRIP

The extent to which your fingers are spread in gripping the racket is a matter of "feel" related to the size of your hand.

"Feel", or "touch", is in your fingers. The important thing is that they—not the palm of your hand—apply the pressure.

Spreading the fingers provides greater leverage for the wrist and forearm action in the final hitting of the ball, but closer grouping probably facilitates better swinging of the racket to build up racket head speed prior to this final action. It is interesting to note that Geoff Hunt's grip indicates a spread of fingers with about 2.5cm (1in) of the handle protruding below the hand, while Mahmoud Kerim (the Egyptian who was World Open Champion for many years prior to Hashim Khan's takeover) held the end of the handle in the palm of his hand. Kerim had a beautiful swing but his rhythm was upset by Hashim's pace to the ball and quicker stroking, which indicates a serious weakness in that Kerim's grip lacked leverage.

Essential features of a good grip are:
1. It never varies with different strokes.
2. The "V" formed by the thumb and forefinger

The striker (above) is in the ideal position to watch the ball and stroke it accurately. His knees are well bent, his head and eyes are down towards the ball, and his racket head is up. The striker (above left) has barely bent his knees and gets to the ball by bending his back and dropping the racket head. This inevitably results in bad balance and unsafe stroke-making.

rests a little to the left of the centre on the top of the handle when the racket face is vertical.

3. The racket is carried and used with the forearm at approximately a right-angle to the handle. The racket must not be allowed to fall towards a position that makes it appear to be an extension of the forearm.

4. The real pressure is felt in the fingers rather than the palm.

5. If pressure is applied to the end of the racket to press it down, the palm of the hand will resist this pressure and the end of the handle will not slip away from the palm.

6. A reliable test of your grip is that if you push your arm out away from yourself horizontally the racket head should be cocked up vertically.

It is advisable to have the same grip for both backhand and forehand.

THE KNEES

In squash you must bend your knees a lot more than you do in tennis because the ball rises less and you must hit it at a much lower level. In fact, you must get well down. (See above.)

If you bend your knees you are able to maintain the correct angular relationship between the racket and forearm, and this is conducive to more accurate play. In addition, your eyes are more along the line of flight of the ball as it comes towards you, which gives you a better sight of it. Finally, you can recover more quickly to the centre from a bent knees position.

A lot of errors made in squash are caused by players standing with their knees almost stiff. Get right down and space your feet to maintain balance and permit exchange of body weight.

YES

NO

The striker (above) positions herself comfortably away from the ball so she can reach for it freely and "stay on it" until the stroke is made. The striker (above left) moves too close to the ball for a free stroke. Her consequent cramped action causes her to turn her body and/or lift her head in making the shot, either of which can cause errors.

THE FEET AND BODY

The position of the feet and body in making a squash stroke is very important—and more varied than in tennis. Body pivot is more pronounced due to the number of directions in which a ball may have to be hit in relation to a given foot position. You have to go back consistently to retrieve shots that have passed you. This calls for shots which are generally not possible in tennis.

The necessity for correct positioning of the feet and body is particularly apparent in backhand shots. If you stand facing the front wall to hit a shot on your backhand, you will find it impossible to hit the ball from the moment it becomes level with your body and even if you hit it earlier your backswing will be severely restricted. If you commence with your right shoulder towards the front wall (as you should) you will be able to make a full backswing and hit the ball freely at any time prior to it passing out of reach behind you.

If it is apparent that the ball will pass your position before you can hit it, turn your right shoulder further around so that your back either faces or nearly faces the front wall and you will find that you can move and swing freely with your back still facing in that direction. If you do not turn your body, your movement to the ball will be restricted and you will not be able to hit freely at the ball once it gets behind you.

The same principles apply to forehand shots. You must stand side-on to the front wall for shots that don't pass you and turn around more and more as you are forced to strike behind your original position.

You can also stand comfortably in either of the back corners with your back to the front wall and hit the ball into any of the four corners of the court with perfect freedom and plenty of pace. An added advantage of this position is that your body conceals your racket from your opponent at the time when its

When retrieving a ball from a back corner it is often necessary to play it with the back turned to the front wall. This striker demonstrates how the ball may be hit to any one of the four corners from this position.

movement would give him a clue as to the direction in which you intend to hit the ball.

The position of the feet can be considered in relation to the positioning of the body. If you are standing side-on to the front wall to hit a ball level with or in front of your body, the foot nearest the front wall should be closer to the side wall you are facing than is the other foot. It is advisable to accentuate this stance in practice so that under pressure you will always have the front foot in this position.

When you turn your body around further to reach a ball that has passed you, the position of the feet is the same in relation to the body in its new position as when your body was side-on to the front wall.

Remember, proper positioning of the body and feet enables you to play most shots with a consistent swing in relation to your body—a most important aid to accuracy.

A "GROOVED" ACTION

The racket head is swung in a vertical plane during the backswing, but the grip then swings the racket into a horizontal plane so that the racket head does not fall below the hand. The transition from backswing to forward movement is continuous. The racket head must never be checked at this stage, but accelerated as it is swung out behind the hand and down.

It is most important that when you stand at a given spot on the court to hit a ball coming from a given direction you always have your feet in the same place and use exactly the same backswing, no matter where you intend to hit the ball to. Your feet will be in different positions only according to where you are on the court and from where the ball comes. But for each such circumstance you must choose one position for your feet from which you can hit the ball to any place on the court.

The reason for this is that the squash court is very small and you cannot afford to "telegraph" your intentions in any way. So as it is possible to make any shot to any position on the court while having your feet in the same place and using the same backswing, you should try to master this. If you have a "grooved" action until your racket approaches the ball no opponent can anticipate your shot and move to it early. Set out to build your stroke play around this theory.

THE SWING

The swing of the racket which constitutes a stroke is one continuous and smooth action aimed at providing maximum racket head speed at point of contact with minimum muscular effort and minimum margin for error. The full swing should be smooth and co-ordinated, generally with a large arc of the hand and racket head.

The clearest way to teach stroke play here is to describe the swing in two separate components, but remember they *must* be joined and employed finally as one simple continuous action.

A tennis stroke is a single movement swinging at a roughly constant horizontal level from behind the body, around and through the ball. The constant level should line up as early as possible with the point at which the racket contacts the ball and thus minimise error. The heavy, tight tennis racket and the high pressure tennis ball ensure adequate pace from the stroke.

This horizontal level is also desirable in squash, with more accent on bending the knees to lower the level of the racket to the height of the ball. However it is necessary to generate greater racket head speed at impact if the ball is to be hit with pace. This generation of speed is started in a wind-up in the vertical backswing much like a golf stroke or the action of a whip, with the impetus being maintained and increased in the horizontal forward movement by a greater emphasis on forearm and wrist action than in the tennis stroke.

Most players do not swing the racket sufficiently behind the body to develop maximum racket head speed or accuracy in the forward movement. For this reason it is best to learn this area of the swing before moving to the full swing. It is also the best way for young children to play until they are strong enough to use a full squash swing correctly.

Limited Horizontal Swing (Horizontal Forward Movement)

The limited horizontal swing starts with the racket head behind and around the body from the ultimate point of contact with the ball. The forearm and racket are held in a horizontal plane so that the racket head is "open". The racket is at an approximate right angle to the forearm and the elbow is bent, forward of the hand and well free of the body.

Start forward with your elbow bent and leading and, as you come round, gradually straighten your elbow and reach for the ball, hitting well through it in the direction you want it to go. The real strength of this movement is in the forearm, wrist and hand. The action of the forehand is similar to that used when you are throwing a stone to make it skim quickly across water.

FOREHAND

BACKHAND

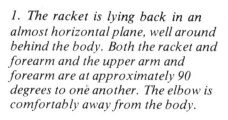

1. The racket is lying back in an almost horizontal plane, well around behind the body. Both the racket and forearm and the upper arm and forearm are at approximately 90 degrees to one another. The elbow is comfortably away from the body.

2. With the elbow leading, the racket head is brought around on a horizontal plane with the single determination to get it to and through the ball ahead of the hand. Pace and power are in the forearm, wrist and hand, and weight is transferring to the front foot.

3. The speed generated by the gradual straightening of the elbow and the bringing forward of the racket head is near its peak. Weight is fully on the front foot, the knees are bent, the head is perfectly still and the eyes are kept on the ball. The body is kept out of the stroke.

REAR VIEW   *FRONT VIEW*

LIMITED HORIZONTAL SWING

4. Contact with the ball is made in a free horizontal hitting action. The knees are well bent, weight is on the front foot, the eyes are on the ball and the racket is reaching out to meet the ball slightly ahead of the front foot on the forehand and a clear 40cm (15in) ahead of it on the backhand for a down-the-wall shot. The arm is now straight.

5. The racket head follows through horizontally until it points at the front wall. The elbow then starts to bend again to allow the racket to flow up and around freely. Weight is still on the front foot and the position of the head is altered only by turning to watch the ball. (Note that in steps 2-5 there is no change in body position other than is necessary to allow free flow of the racket.)

6. The racket finishes the follow-through over the left shoulder (forehand) or right shoulder (backhand). A quick move back to the centre-court position has been started by pushing off with the front foot and raising the head and body.

The racket head in this horizontal swing not only has the acceleration normally promoted by a straight arm swing, but also the generation of speed caused by a 90-degree elbow angle and a 90-degree angle lay-back of the racket by the forearm and wrist each being brought back to a virtual straight line before impact. There is a similarity in mechanics between this and the generation of racket head speed in a power serve in tennis.

You must not take up a position too close to the ball when commencing your stroke. Stand away from it and then reach freely to hit it. Note that the point of your elbow will be pointing at the floor on impact with the ball in both backhand and forehand strokes.

When making your forward movement it is vital to think solely of getting the racket head to and through the ball ahead of your hand. You should lead with the elbow, forcing the forearm, wrist and hand to accelerate the speed of the racket head. Provided the shoulders and body are kept out of the action you'll achieve a surprising racket head speed. If you were to bring them in after the forward movement commenced you would block the shot and reduce speed.

The hand and racket head are in fact almost in line at impact, with the racket head then going quickly ahead. However, the mental incentive must be that no matter how much power is exerted by the forearm, wrist and hand to get themselves forward, the racket head must beat them to the line of impact.

You must follow through with your racket head after first contact with the ball. Many players tend to regard first contact as the end of the effective stroke and pull their rackets quickly away from the ball, with resultant errors.

To transfer the full pace from the racket head to the ball you should think of hitting through it and out after it. If you find you are not following through adequately, make a conscious effort to put your head down towards the ball and hit a full 30-50cm (12-18in) through it until you have corrected the fault.

The combination of hitting through the ball with the forearm and racket head accelerating while the shoulder and body are no more than passively pulled around by the stroke allows your follow through to be free and unrestrained. Your racket head should follow out some 30-50cm (12-18in) after the ball, then swing around and, with the elbow finally bending at about the time the racket is pointing at the front wall, finish in a near vertical position to the left (forehand) or right (backhand) of your head.

Provided you have followed through correctly the latter part of your swing should be automatic and effortless, and not obstruct your opponent.

It is wise to play only with this limited horizontal stroke for about two months to inculcate the habit of generating maximum racket head speed in the horizontal forward movement and to be sure that you never lose sight of the fact that this is the hitting area in your full swing.

The forearm and firm wrist movement does not alter the approximate 90-degree relationship between forearm and racket at impact.

Throughout the stroke push your left arm out and away from your body in the manner most suited to maintaining perfect balance. For a forehand it is best to point your arm towards the ball early in the swing to get your weight forward.

The main reasons for mastering the limited horizontal swing before attempting the full swing are:

1. It is impossible to use this swing effectively when facing the front wall so it becomes second nature to face the side wall while hitting.
2. The action of swinging around the body and gradually straightening the elbow ensures that you reach freely for the ball (and therefore do not stand too close to it).
3. If boasting is learnt while using this swing the racket head will be adjusted for the boast without dropping to a different arc.
4. You learn to consistently hit through the ball with the racket head slightly open and not drop or lift it while doing so.
5. By meeting the ball in front of the front foot and keeping the body out of the shot you achieve the best racket head speed.
6. You learn to hit in the safe horizontal plane and this later becomes a feature of your full swing.

It is interesting to note that when an experienced player is having trouble with his stroke play, a period spent reverting to the limited horizontal swing generally has extremely beneficial results.

The Full Swing

The full swing comes from linking the limited horizontal swing with a backswing wind-up. The link up with the forward movement must start momentarily at a higher level than the starting point in the horizontal forward movement. However, the racket drops quickly to the ultimate horizontal plane and forearm and wrist power bring the racket head at maximum pace ahead of the hand at impact as practised in the limited horizontal swing.

Always start any stroke with your racket in a vertical position. Be comfortable, with your elbow a

FOREHAND

BACKHAND

1. The player is moving in to meet the ball. The racket is vertical and ready to start the swing, even though one further step is yet to be taken.

2. During the final step to meet the ball the backswing commences, with the elbow going back and the racket head barely moving prior to whipping back with great acceleration. Weight is not yet on the front foot.

3. The racket head is thrown back, gaining speed. As it passes back over the elbow, the weight is transferring to the front foot.

REAR VIEW

FULL SWING STRAIGHT DRIVE

4. The racket is coming down behind the body and the elbow is leading the forward movement, creating a whiplash effect on the racket head.

5. The position now reached is almost the same as for the commencement of a horizontal swing, except that the backswing has already created pace in the racket head. The action now becomes as for the limited horizontal swing, with the player's one thought being to get the racket head to the ball ahead of the fast-moving hand. The body is kept out of the shot.

6. In moving to the ball, tremendous pace must be generated in the racket head to get it to and through the ball ahead of the hand.

FRONT VIEW

7. Contact with the ball is made in a free horizontal hitting action. The knees are well bent, weight is on the front foot, and the racket is reaching out to meet the ball slightly ahead of the front foot on the forehand and a clear 40cm (15in) ahead of it on the backhand. The arm is now straight.

8. The racket head follows through horizontally until it points at the front wall. The elbow then starts to bend again to allow the racket to flow up and around freely. Weight is still on the front foot and the position of the head is altered only by turning to watch the ball. (Note that in steps 6-8 there is no change in body position other than is necessary to allow free flow of the racket.)

9. The racket finishes the follow-through over the left shoulder (forehand) or right shoulder (backhand). A quick move back to the centre-court position has been started by pushing off with the front foot and raising the head and body.

FOREHAND

BACKHAND

Contact with the ball is made a clear 30 cm (12in) in front of the front foot for the forehand or a clear 60cm (24in) for the backhand. The arm is closer to the body and the racket follows through further across the body than in a straight drive. Positions 1-6 inclusive of the Full Swing Straight Drive (see pages 37-38) apply identically to this shot.

FULL SWING CROSS-COURT DRIVE

little out from your body and a little lower than your hand and the racket vertical and opposite your right shoulder.

The first movement is to turn the hips a little and take the elbow back and out from the body (press it back on the backhand). The racket and forearm remain at approximate right angles to one another. In this initial part of the movement the racket head falls behind and slowly leaves its original position to be ready to commence its large arc and build-up of speed. The turn of the hips enables you to swing freely. The elbow moves back and out from the body, and the forearm then comes over and past the elbow to throw the hand and racket well out behind the body in a big arc with the racket head rapidly accelerating.

The upper body must be allowed to move freely, but apart from the initial brief hip movement no attempt should be made to use the body or shoulders as a hitting medium. Racket head pace is obtained through the firm movement of the arm, perhaps with some use of the shoulder as a fulcrum but basically with the main movement in the backswing being started and revolving around the elbow. The forearm adds its effect by turning over and laying the racket back on a near horizontal plane at the end of

the backswing, then taking over the full momentum of the backswing and adding to it by forcing the racket head on a horizontal plane to reach the ball ahead of the hand. In other words, the considerable momentum arising from the whip of the racket head in the backswing is taken over and to it is added the momentum which you have already developed in the limited horizontal swing.

With a smooth action giving full play to continuous racket head acceleration you will find that the ball will come off your racket with great pace and you will have a feeling of surprise at how little effort you have put into it.

So in making the full swing, remember:

1. Face the side wall with the racket vertical and opposite your right shoulder. While making your stroke push the left arm out away from your body in the manner most suited to maintaining perfect balance, which is essential to good stroke-making.
2. Start your backswing early (when moving quickly to the ball this will be before you have placed both feet for the shot).
3. The first movement is with the hips and elbow to ensure a full and comfortable swing with the elbow moving back and away from the body.

4. With a continuing smooth action throw your forearm and racket out behind you over the fulcrum of the elbow so the racket (at approximately a right angle to your forearm) comes down in a position well around your body as you start your strong forearm and wrist movement forward.

5. From the time this strong forward movement is started (with the pace generated from the whip of the backswing), bend your knees to adjust to the height of the ball and concentrate on getting the racket head ahead of the hand.

6. Practise and practise until the swing becomes second nature and you are playing the stroke as one continuous, smooth movement which is automatic, accurate and powerful.

Note: From the time your racket starts to move from the vertical position it must never be checked.

When you are hitting a drive across court you follow the same line in your backswing as for a shot down the wall but on your forward movement you bring the racket head in closer to your feet and take it forward to hit the ball well out in front of your feet. This means that the racket head generally falls a little below the hand, but you still have an angle of about 120 degrees between your forearm and the racket and you bend your knees and hit the ball in front of your feet and follow through in the direction you are aiming.

RACKET HEAD POSITION

In making an orthodox stroke it is important to do everything possible to hit the ball with the racket head at least as high as the wrist at the point of contact. Start with the racket vertical and your forearm almost making a right angle with it and make every effort to maintain this angle as you reach out to meet the ball. This keeps the racket head above the wrist and enables you to hit the ball with greater accuracy. There are times when you must hit a ball near the floor, but even then you should not drop the racket head down away from the wrist. Instead, bend your knees and drop your hand down too, so that your racket head is still being held at the required angle to your forearm and has not dropped to look as if the racket is a continuation of your forearm.

So, keep the racket head at an approximate right angle to the forearm both in carrying it and using it to hit the ball. Although there are times when the ball is so low that it is impossible to carry this out fully, keep as close to it as you can. The occasions when you can not maintain this angle must be regarded as the exception rather than the rule and you should bend your knees where necessary to minimise the variation.

CONTACT WITH THE BALL

A squash shot is basically a flat shot. The fact that you hit forward along the ball's line of flight automatically "opens" the face of your racket a little in the "hitting area" (see pictures, page 44), but you do not consciously apply cut or slice.

You should never play over the ball in squash (i.e. "close" the racket head) as is the tendency in tennis. Allow your racket to "open" as you follow through, but think in terms of hitting a flat shot along the line of flight of the ball after it is hit, with the racket head at least as high as your wrist, and you will automatically hit an orthodox squash shot. Never use top spin. Slice will be applied in certain more delicate shots, some of which are mentioned later.

POSITION OF THE BALL WHEN HIT

This is one of the most important points in hitting a ball because it has a great effect on determining whether you can time a ball well and hit it faster without apparent effort—in other words, apply pace without "telegraphing" your intentions.

Timing and pace come largely from hitting the ball early. For maximum pace hit the ball in front of the front foot, with your weight predominantly on that foot. If you get out on the court by yourself and hit the ball up and down, gradually reaching out further for it, you will find a position at which you get maximum pace with minimum effort. Champions hit normal basic shots with little effort, but the ball travels faster than when hit by most players using every effort. This ability comes from smooth swinging, expert timing and picking the correct position in front of their feet to make contact with the ball.

The relative position of the ball when hit is further ahead on the backhand than on the forehand. This is due to the mechanical effect of using the front shoulder for the backhand and the back shoulder for the forehand.

Provided you get your body weight well forward, a guide to the position of the ball when hit is: on the forehand a little in front of the front foot for down-the-wall shots and about 30cm (12in) in front for cross-court shots. On the backhand about 40cm (15in) in front of the front foot for down-the-wall shots and about 60cm (24in) for cross-court shots.

YES

YES

The striker (above) commences his swing while still approaching the ball. His body is facing the side wall and his feet are correctly placed to make his stroke. He uses a full effortless swing (above right) which brings the racket through on a safe horizontal plane. The striker (right) is making one of the most common and serious faults in squash today. His feet are settled in the final position before his stroke gets under way, which means he'll tend to rush his stroke. He will hit his forehand with his body facing the front wall, feet wrongly placed, knees barely bent and his weight on the back foot. This results in a small arc of the racket head (far right) which requires great effort to achieve racket head pace. His swing will contain a minimum horizontal plane and the racket will contact the ball opposite the back foot. This imposes heavy strain on his arm and shoulder and makes him particularly prone to making mistakes under pressure because he lacks safety and consistency in his shots.

NO

NO

John Fairfax

Australia's world champions Geoff Hunt (left) and Heather McKay (right) show the ideal forehand technique. As they move in to meet the ball they bring the racket head around in a horizontal plane from well behind the body. The elbow is leading, weight is on the front foot, the knees are well bent and the left arm is extended to assist balance. Tremendous racket head speed will be generated in hitting the ball, which will be met opposite the front foot.

By hitting the ball in front of yourself you can keep it down. In fact, the further in front you meet the ball, the more you can make it sit down. Even with a smash hit from high up the ball will sit down if you hit it far enough in front of yourself. The former world champion Mahmoud Kerim had an amazing ability to smash a ball and make it bounce a couple of times before it reached his opponent. He did this simply by hitting the ball well in front.

As you can see, there are several advantages in meeting the ball well forward. You time it well and with your weight forward get maximum pace with minimum effort. As you take the ball earlier you make your opponent run earlier, and when you are hitting hard you can make the ball sit down and not come off the back wall. Hitting the ball in front of yourself also makes it easier to hit a cross-court drive with severity yet with the same backswing as a drive down the wall.

In match play you must maintain balance to hit the ball in front of yourself. If you can do this you will be applying pressure. If your opponent knocks you off balance to the extent that you cannot hit the ball in front of yourself, you will lose pressure and your opponent will be applying pressure to you.

You cannot get maximum pressure into your game if you hit off the back foot. You cannot hit the ball as hard, low or accurately in terms of length as you can when you hit off the front foot.

Of course, sometimes you will be forced to hit shots off your back foot simply because you won't have time to move into a correct position. Nonetheless if you want to be the one who applies pressure most consistently *always* fight to get in position to hit the ball off the correct foot and in front of you. Even if you do not succeed fully, you will get touch, weight and as much forward balance as possible into the shot and maintain pressure on your opponent.

With practice and training, you'll find you can make nearly all your strokes correctly and thereby force your opponent into errors.

Always planning to hit the ball in front of yourself also gives you more margin if your opponent's speed surprises you—at worst you should hit the ball level with your body. If you were originally intending to hit the ball level with your body and he surprised you with speed you would be forced back on to your heels.

In good match play you are consistently forced to hit the ball on the fall at about the same height as the top of the "tin" (i.e. approximately knee height). This is a good height to take a ball and hit it accurately, with both length and pressure. In fact you should seek to hit it there because at this height the possibility of error is smallest and good length can be most consistently maintained.

FOREHAND

BACKHAND

1. In backswing.   *2. Point of contact.*   *3. Follow-through.*

Former world champion and classical stroke-maker Roshan Khan demonstrates the straight drive. Much of Australian technique was modelled on his style.

FOREHAND

BACKHAND

BACKHAND

Roshan Khan (left and centre) and Hashim Khan (right) demonstrate the point of contact on a cross-court drive. Hashim won the World Open Championship seven times in the 1950s.

The benefit of hitting at knee height, however, must always be balanced against the benefit of quick interception of the ball at any height to bustle your opponent. If, for example, to take the ball at knee height necessitated you needlessly retreating from the centre court and thereby losing the pressure you'd put on your opponent—don't do it. You should *always* cut his shots off early provided you can do so smoothly and stroke accurately.

LENGTH AND WHERE TO AIM

Although length and where to aim are not strictly a part of stroke play, they are so closely allied to it that they should be introduced and practised from this point.

For the purposes of this chapter the term length is considered as a function of pace as well as distance.

In practice length has no significance unless the ball reaches its objective. The term is also used here only in relation to shots hit deep in the court although in other circumstances it could apply to lobs, drop shots or boasts.

In driving a ball towards the back or side walls it is of good length if it has enough pace to: (a) beat the opponent completely and not give him a chance to hit it on the rebound from the wall, or (b) force him to hit it just before it reaches the wall because he cannot hit it earlier and fears the consequences of attempting a shot off the rebound.

The point at which to aim on the front wall to achieve a good length shot depends not only on pace but also on position and height from which the ball is hit, the type of ball used and the temperature of both the court and ball. It can vary from 10cm (4in) above the tin to near the cut line (the centre line on the front wall). *No* hard hit ball should be aimed lower than 10cm (4in) above the tin.

You must find the front wall spots that achieve a good length shot for each position on the court. If you are hitting from the back of a cold court on a cold night you may have to aim up towards the cut line. If you are hitting from well forward on the court in warm conditions and you are a strong hitter you may have to aim 10cm(4in) above the tin. If you are hitting from high up you will have to hit higher than normal on the front wall. When hitting from knee height back in the court, it is generally essential to aim sufficiently high to be certain that the ball will hit the floor behind the short line, perhaps even deeper.

You must simply experiment with shots from all parts of the court to decide where to aim to achieve good length.

The striker (right) has her body forward and weight on the front foot. This enables her to hit the ball hard and low so that it will not bounce off the back wall. The striker (below) is leaning back to strike the ball and her weight is on the back foot. Her stroke will lack power and the ball will tend to lift.

YES

NO

THE SERVICE

The ideal service brings the ball into play with minimum risk of a "double fault", is safe from attack and puts hand-out on the defensive.

A good player who is determined to attack your service will attempt to volley the ball either before it hits the side wall or immediately after it has hit that wall. He will do everything possible to upset the accuracy and effectiveness of your planned service strategy. Hence you should be equipped with more than one form of service and be in a position to switch from one to another without prior warning.

The best basic serve is a semi-lob made with your body facing the forehand wall and struck at about eye height and about the distance of an outstretched arm. The pictures of Roshan Khan (above right) clearly show aspects of the action to be used.

Roshan's racket head moves from the position shown, perhaps rising and moving out a little, and strikes under and a little across the ball, throwing it up into the air and imparting a little slice for control. The ball is hit high to a point well up the front wall and rebounds higher still but safely below the ceiling on any first-class court.

The ball from this service should rebound from the front wall to strike the side wall approximately level with the back line of the service box and sufficiently high to stop hand-out from volleying it before it hits that wall. You must make the ball fall sufficiently below the "out of court" line to ensure safety. If stroked with the correct touch and not volleyed by hand-out, it should drop deep in the court and force him to play a defensive shot before or after it hits the back wall.

This service is a mechanical shot and you should always position yourself in the same way and make contact with the ball in the same place to gain consistent accuracy. Do not simply walk into the service box and use a semi-lob or lob service without correctly positioning yourself or you may serve out-of-court and lose your hand.

If hand-in is upsetting your rhythm or accuracy by offensive volleying, switch to a serve from the same position and hit about head high but hard and low to near the cut line.

The efficiency of this faster service lies in its surprise and safety. How to use it depends a great deal on your opponent. You must not allow him to get to your serve quickly—by volleying, for example—as you will not have time to take your centre position before he puts you under serious attack. You should vary your direction to keep him guessing.

Always keep the following points firmly in mind when you are making this service:

A front view (left) and side view (right) of Roshan Khan demonstrating the correct semi-lob service.

1. The ball should hit the side wall before your opponent can play it. The fast service will hit that wall lower than will a lofted service and must not bounce too far across the court or too far out from the back wall as your opponent would then have a clear half-court to attack.

2. The further your opponent stands back, the deeper and lower your service can hit the side wall—and this is to your advantage.

3. If your opponent is pressing forward to volley your service before or soon after it hits the side wall, serve a fast one straight at him a few times to make him move back closer to the centre. Serving down the centre line in such circumstances is generally not wise as you cannot take the centre position yourself and he has the opportunity to hit a winner if he recovers his position quickly enough.

4. Always know where your opponent is standing, even when you face the side wall to hit your forehand service.

A lob service is played by facing the front wall and bringing the racket under and upwards to strike the ball in front of the body and at a low level. The ball is lofted high to the front wall and then rises as high as the ceiling will allow, finally falling on the side wall at a distance from the back wall such that it will barely rebound from the back wall on the first bounce. If played perfectly it is the best of all services, but it is risky in almost any player's hands and too many points are lost in competition by the ball going out of court. It is also impossible to use on a court with a low ceiling and because of the low point of contact it is difficult to change suddenly from it to a fast service.

Although a semi-lob service is usually played as a forehand stroke from the forehand court, it can be played on the backhand from that court. As well as

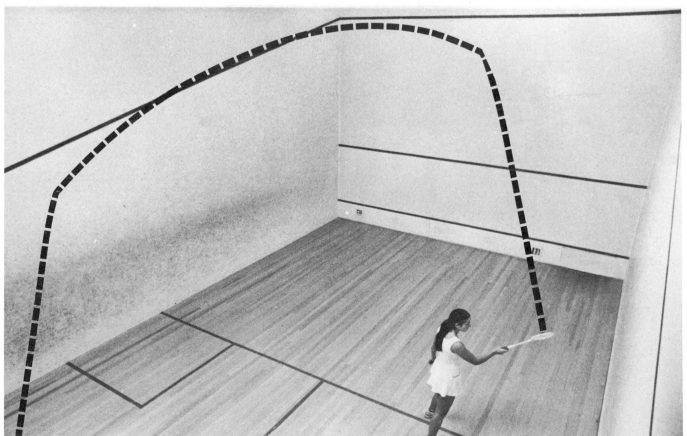

A high, safe semi-lob service played from the backhand court (top above) and the forehand court (above). This serve is difficult to attack.

FOREHAND

BACKHAND

1. The player is positioned in the angle of the "T" opposite to her opponent, who is striking the ball from near the front wall. Her knees are bent, the racket is vertical, her feet are turned slightly towards her opponent, and her eyes are on both the ball and her opponent's stroke so that she is ready to move instantly.

2. As soon as the player knows where the ball is going she takes her racket back for a smooth, powerful volley and turns her hips and feet to take up the correct feet and body position to hit the ball.

3. Contact with the ball is made in a firm hitting action, with weight on the front foot. The ball is met a little ahead of the front foot on the forehand and well ahead of it on the backhand, and is volleyed deep down the near side wall.

FRONT VIEW

VOLLEY DOWN THE WALL

4. The racket follows a near horizontal plane until it points towards the front wall, and will finish over the shoulder as in all full shots. The player is well placed in the centre-court area to move to her next shot and her main concern now is to give her opponent a clear path to the ball.

enabling you to use the same angle and trajectory for services from each court, this feature has the advantage that you are always facing hand-out so you can watch him and take your position at the centre after service with the utmost ease.

Whichever service you use, remember, the essential feature is that it should not allow the receiver to attack. He should not be able to volley it before it hits the side wall or hit a forcing length shot from its rebound from the back wall.

THE VOLLEY

This is an essential shot in putting pressure on your opponent and taking advantage of his wildly hit or weak shots. Part of your aim in moving your opponent about is to force him to make a weak shot which you can cut off by volley or otherwise for a winner.

The manner of making a volley depends on whether the ball comes to you quickly or slowly and whether you wish to drop it short, slam it into the nick or hit it the full length of the court.

If the ball comes to you quickly there is little time for the extreme accuracy of stroking a delicate shot just over the tin into the nick. Here the "percentage" shot is a firm hit with a good backswing and strong follow-through to a safe margin above the tin and sufficiently high for the ball to reach one of the back corners. Start with the racket held vertically and move quickly. A firmly hit shot to the front nick can be used if your opponent is deep and the ball comes to you in the right position.

If you have more time to make your stroke you have more options. You can give yourself maximum time by being well positioned, holding your racket head vertical, standing on your toes and watching your opponent hit the ball.

In quick volleys you have less chance than in any other shot of attaining correct hitting position, but when you do the shots fall almost into the categories of drives, nick shots, smashes and drop shots, albeit from varied heights. The same principles of feet position, facing the side wall, backswing, follow-through and so forth apply and, apart from "drive" volleys, slice will always be imparted to some degree.

"Stop" or "drop" volleys should be practised, although used only when the shot is "on". The margin is fine, but the prize is generally a point.

Remember, if hitting from a height the ball must be aimed well above the tin to reach the back wall. Alternatively, hit a volley well out in front of yourself and near the tin and even a firmly hit ball will sit down.

Practice volleys assiduously because they are often the winning shot in a rally designed to throw up a weak shot. When you have set the trap be ready and, above all, be in position with your racket held vertically.

Emergency Volleying

When your opponent is hitting from the front of the court he can hit the ball very hard and even when you are in a position to volley it you can be forced to do so earlier than expected. You may not have time to adjust your feet and body and swing your racket as for a classical volley but you must do the best you can to attempt a winner.

Take your racket back quickly and step sideways, turning your hips so that your body is half-facing the side wall. However, stop the movement of your other foot across to concentrate on making a quick shot. This means you must stop your backswing, say half-way back, push with your back foot to get whatever "forward balance" you can, meet the ball as early as possible in the circumstances, and make sure you follow-through. The arc of your hand will be very small and you must use the utmost power from your forearm and wrist.

So, when you don't have time to make a full stroke concentrate on the racket meeting the ball and following through and on achieving as much "forward balance" as you can.

There will be times in general play when you will be forced to similar emergency measures, but should this happen too often you must improve your positional play and watch the ball more closely.

THE BOAST

A boast is hit with the feet in the same position as for a hard down-the-wall shot. Your racket starts from the vertical position and follows the same groove into the horizontal plane as the down-the-wall shot until the hand is approaching the line of the right side of your body. At this stage the racket head is diverted from the path of a down-the-wall shot by keeping the hand ahead of it, lowering it very slightly, and opening it so that the ball is struck with an open face towards the desired point on the side wall.

Normally the ball is struck behind the point at which it would be struck for a down-the-wall shot— about 30cm (12in) behind the front foot for the forehand and level with the front foot for the backhand. The weight is still well on the front foot and racket head pace is only slightly diminished.

50

FOREHAND

BACKHAND

1. The player is positioned in the angle of the "T" opposite to her opponent, who is striking the ball from near the front wall. Her knees are bent, the racket is vertical, her feet are turned slightly towards her opponent, and her eyes are on both the ball and her opponent's stroke so that she is ready to move instantly.

FRONT VIEW

EMERGENCY VOLLEY

2. Surprised by the pace of her opponent's shot, the player has only enough time to step sideways with her right foot (forehand) or left foot (backhand) and turn her hips, which brings the foot back and the body to an angle of 45 degrees. There is no time to move the other foot, so the backswing must be shortened according to how much time is available.

3. The player gets "forward balance" by pushing with her back foot to meet the ball as far forward as she can manage. As she is forced to make the shot with a small arc of the hand and racket head, she uses the strength of her wrist and forearm to get the necessary power and volleys the ball deep down the near side wall.

4. The racket follows a near horizontal plane, and to ensure power and accuracy the player must try to follow through as fully as in a classical volley (see page 49). The player is well placed in the centre-court area to move to her next shot and her main concern now is to give her opponent a clear path to the ball.

FOREHAND

BACKHAND

1. The player is moving in to meet the ball. The racket is vertical and ready to start the swing, even though one further step is yet to be taken.

2. During the final step to meet the ball the backswing commences, with the elbow going back and the racket head barely moving prior to whipping back with great acceleration. Weight is not yet on the front foot.

3. The racket head is thrown back, gaining speed. As it passes back over the elbow, the weight is transferring to the front foot.

REAR VIEW

BOAST

4. The racket is coming down behind the body and the elbow is leading the forward movement, creating a whiplash effect on the racket head.

5. The position now reached is almost the same as for the commencement of a horizontal swing, except that the backswing has already created pace in the racket head. The action now becomes as for the limited horizontal swing, with the player's one thought being to bring the racket head around to catch up with the fast-moving hand. The body is now kept out of the shot.

6. In moving into the ball, much pace must be generated in the racket head to get it to and through the ball a little behind the hand.

FRONT VIEW

53

7. Contact with the ball is made in a free horizontal hitting action, with the knees well bent and the weight on the front foot. The racket head is lowered slightly and its face is opened to meet the ball a little behind the hand to direct it to the desired point on the side wall. The ball is met a little behind the front foot (forehand) or ahead of the front foot (backhand). The arm is now straight.

8. The racket head follows through horizontally until it points at the front wall. The elbow then starts to bend again to allow the racket to flow up and around freely. Weight is still on the front foot and the position of the head is altered only by turning to watch the ball. (Note that in steps 6-8 there is no change in body position other than is necessary to allow free flow of the racket.)

9. The racket finishes the follow-through over the left (forehand) or right (backhand) shoulder. A quick move back to the centre-court position has been started by pushing off with the front foot and raising the head and body.

Former world amateur champion and noted stroke player Cam Nancarrow demonstrates a forehand boast. His knees are bent, he has opened the face of his racket and he will keep his hand ahead of the racket head on contact with the ball.

A good boast does not bounce back off the opposite side wall. Its second bounce should be before or into the nick of that wall. If this is not so, the ball must be struck to hit the near-side wall further towards the front wall to correct the fault.

When making a boast near the wall in the forecourt it is possible to meet the ball at a point not visible to an opponent placed in the centre of the court. Provided your backswing is consistent for all shots, you can in many cases use the element of surprise with this shot.

A "reverse" boast (i.e. one hit on to the side wall opposite to that which you face) must be hit close to, and in front of, your feet—more so than with a cross-court drive.

A boast hit on to the back wall first is as a rule a purely defensive shot, but Kerim used it effectively to retrieve length shots rather than rush to retrieve them with normal boasts from the back of the court. He was exceptionally accurate and bent low to hit the ball so that it rebounded from the back wall over his shoulders, struck the front wall near the diagonally opposite corner and hugged the side wall as it bounced back. So, although defensive, this shot is worth practising as it enables you to retrieve seemingly impossible shots without undue body effort, regain the centre and have your opponent play from the side wall. For improved safety and positional advantage the ball should hit the front wall high enough to rebound well back from it and near the side wall.

THE DROP SHOT

Drop shots are played from closer to the ball than normal and the stroke always starts with the racket held vertically.

To maximise deception the elbow is taken well back with the hand following as if to commence a full swing, but in fact the racket head barely moves from its original lateral position. The racket remains in the same plane as the forearm (but at a right angle to it) and the racket head drops a little vertically.

FOREHAND

BACKHAND

1. The player has taken a position closer to the path of the ball than she would for a freely hit drive. The elbow is taken back as in the first movement of a full swing to convince the opponent that the ball could be hit firmly to the full length of the court. The racket head, however, barely moves from its original position.

2. The elbow leads forward, and the forearm and racket lean back in the one plane at 90 degrees to one another. The racket is held firmly at the same angle to the forearm throughout the stroke and moves virtually at the same pace as the hand. The forearm and wrist do not turn at all from now on.

3. The elbow remains bent and moves forward and a little across the body. The movement of the hand guides and paces the racket head into the ball. The racket head is lying back and, as it remains in a constant relationship to the hand and forearm, slices under and slightly across the ball. The head is kept well down, the weight is forward and the eyes are fixed on the ball.

FRONT VIEW

DROP SHOT

4. The follow-through is limited, coming across the body as a continuation of the path already established. As the follow-through is slow and relatively restricted, the knees will quickly straighten in the fast recovery action generally necessary after a drop shot.

Note: For a drop shot off a high ball, position 2 is a good point of contact with the ball; for a cross-court drop shot, position 4.

This causes the opponent to stay back to cover a length shot. The elbow is then taken forward well ahead of its original position, with the forearm and racket leaning back in the one plane and the racket head still very close to its original position but poised ready to make a delicate slice under the ball in the forward movement.

The approximate 90-degree angle between racket and forearm is maintained throughout the stroke. Although straightening somewhat, the elbow remains bent throughout and definitely leads the hand and racket in the early part of the forward movement towards the ball.

In this forward movement the forearm, wrist and hand keep the racket head lying back in relation to the hand, thereby preventing acceleration. The racket head is kept on a straight line into the ball by taking the elbow towards the front of the body, which brings the racket head slowly into the ball and into a slicing action as it meets it.

The important thing to keep in mind about the drop shot is that the hand guides the racket, keeps it lying back, and paces the stroke. In playing this shot concentrate on your hand and the racket head.

Your weight must be on the front foot and your head should be down as near to the racket head as is comfortable. With knees bent and all the preliminary movements blended into one smooth action, you must now concentrate on a delicate adjustment of balance and really "stroke" the ball to complete a perfect shot. This is the most delicate stroke in squash.

In many cases where the ball is a little high you may make your shot with the elbow still ahead of the racket head. This means the racket head will not move much at all before meeting the ball.

The delicate stroking of the ball with a slicing action and appropriate touch is vital. The shorter the distance from the front wall, the more delicate the touch and the slower the pace off the racket. Drop shots played from deeper in the court can be played with a firmer stroking.

The follow-through will naturally be much shorter than in a full length shot because the racket head has been held in reasonable check even when stroking the ball. It will be guided by the hand and, to flow smoothly, will follow a path started by the movement of the elbow, that is, it will move across the body soon after completing contact with the ball. A smooth flow at a pace dictated by the hand is the essential factor.

The fact that the ball remains in contact with the racket longer than usual (while slice is being imparted) gives added control. It also gives the ball back-spin which produces a sharp drop when it hits

FOREHAND

1. *Start of stroke.*

2. *Point of contact.*

BACKHAND

3. *Point of contact.*

Former world champions Roshan Khan (left and centre) and Hashim Khan (right) demonstrate drop shots to the near corner. Note how low they crouch.

the front wall. When the shot is to the near-side corner the slice tends to make it cling to the side wall.

The line of flight of the ball after it is hit is a little above the path of the racket head (which is virtually horizontal), and you should resist the temptation to chop downwards.

Drop shots should be aimed to hit the nick or finish on a wall, depending on the position of both the opponent and the ball when hit.

The drop shot requires a great deal of practice and extreme concentration. It must not be "poked", but delicately sliced for success. Above all, bend your knees and be perfectly balanced with your weight well forward when you play it. If you are "popping" your drop shots up the wall you are not getting your weight forward.

When practising, it is wise to alternate length shots with drop shots so you retain the ability to play them both with the same first movement (and a small arc) as a deterrent to any opponent inclined to move forward to cover a possible drop shot.

THE NICK SHOT

In this shot the ball is generally hit hard across court to the front wall (near the side wall), goes down into the nick and, if perfect, shoots across the floor too low to be retrieved. Always make sure the ball hits the side wall on the full.

The nick shot is hit from a ball that is sufficiently high to enable you to hit it downwards at an angle and with a fairly heavy slice. The elbow leads in much the same way as for a tennis serve to achieve pace and the ball is met well forward. Swing the racket a little wide to help with the angle and get well under the ball for consistent accuracy.

The nick shot was first introduced to Australia in 1952 by Hashim Khan. At that time it was popular with many players but due to a combination of the unsuitability of the ball and insufficient understanding of the stroke it was soon more or less discarded.

However in 1957 Hashim and Roshan Khan again demonstrated the stroke here. In match play against one another they both used it very effectively as a killing stroke when the opponent had been manoeuvred out of position to the back of the court but very sparingly when the opponent was in position. The plan was to push the opponent to the back of the court and kill his return quickly into the nick—and very seldom did either of them play the shot when the opponent was well positioned because the penalty of missing against a good player was too serious.

The shot may be used as a variation to surprise an opponent when he has not been pushed deep (for example, an overhead shot to the nick) but whenever it is used the striker must be positioned so he can regain the centre of the court before his opponent reaches the ball.

Australians have spent a lot of time practising this shot and today several top players use it very accurately and effectively from most parts of the court.

But, as invariably happens when a spectacular and killing shot of this nature becomes popular, it has become something of a mania and is used too often from an unsafe strategical position, i.e. when the striker is out of position and could not possibly regain the centre of the court before the opponent

Ken Hiscoe, former Australian and world amateur champion, brings his racket across to meet the ball in a forehand smash across court to the nick. He is renowned for his ability to kill a ball quickly into the nick when his opponent is out of position.

FOREHAND

1. *Moving in to the ball, with the racket coming down from the normal vertical starting position.*

2. *The racket goes under and up.*

CROSS-COURT LOB   *FRONT VIEW*

could reach an inaccurate shot. In top competition nobody is good enough to ignore the possibility that a shot to the nick may not be perfect. Players who do so will be spectacular on their good days and in trouble on the others. The odds are that in serious competition they will not maintain accuracy in this shot unless they wait for the right ball. If they are determined to play for the nick at the earliest moment at all costs they will fall into errors and lose under pressure from a forceful, tight and accurate opponent.

The guiding principle for hitting a nick shot is that you must be able to regain the centre of the court before your opponent can reach the ball. Don't use a nick shot when you are well up towards the front wall unless he is out of position at the back of the court. When he is in position, a shot to the nick should be played only from between a metre or so in front of the short line to about the back of the service boxes unless it is played as a complete surprise shot and therefore catches him moving backwards. Any high bouncing ball or any volley which is suitably clear of the side wall and can be taken from this court position presents a good opportunity to attack an opponent safely, irrespective of his position.

It has become a fetish that this shot must always be hit in a full-blooded manner, however a little less pace with concentration on accuracy may pay better results. The appearance of a full swing can be given before making this shot, which should be sufficient to put your opponent on his heels.

THE DRIVE KILL

This shot is hit hard from forward in the court, the aim being to bounce the ball twice at a great pace before the opponent can reach it. It is generally hit down the near wall perhaps to the nick, but it could also be hit across court if your opponent is out of position.

The drive kill is normally hit well out in front of the body when the ball is at the peak of its bounce and hit down to some centimetres above the tin. Pace to the ball is essential as the success of the shot depends on the opponent being out of position.

THE LOB

Also known as a "toss", the lob is basically used for defensive purposes, but in the hands of a keen strategist it can be used as an offensive shot against impatient opponents who like playing against hard hitters.

The lob is normally made from the forecourt, usually very close to the front wall. The safest, and usually the most effective shot is hit with the action of a lob service and aimed very high so that it goes comfortably out of reach over the opponent's head and strikes the side wall near the diagonally opposite corner with a glancing blow. It then rebounds to bounce near the back wall, leaving the opponent little chance to attack. Due to the height of the shot you have ample time to regain the central position.

3. The racket continues up to the point of contact with the ball.

4. The racket moves upwards in the follow-through.

5. The follow-through finishes over the left shoulder.

Note: The hitting trajectory throughout this stroke is under and up.

This shot is nowhere near as risky as a lob service and with practice great accuracy can be achieved.

In certain cases, particularly when you are too late to lob across court, you can benefit by lobbing high and hugging the side wall but the risks are greater than the cross-court shot because it is easier to hit the ball over the side wall line and difficult to keep it close to the wall.

EYES ON THE BALL

Keeping your eyes on the ball sounds elementary but in squash it is vitally important—you must *never* take your eyes off it. The racket head is small, so you must watch the ball right on to it. Even among good players, the greatest percentage of unnecessary mistakes is caused by taking the eyes off the ball. So whenever you are playing badly remember, *eyes on the ball.*

THE IMPORTANCE OF PRACTICE

It is of utmost importance to develop effective stroke play early in your career and the only way to do that is through practice—both by yourself and with others.

If you are not in a position to spend a lot of time on a court on your own you can improvise. Clear out your garage, put a board across the end wall at the height of the tin on a squash court, then stand outside the garage, not inside, and practise hitting the ball up and down, remembering to move your feet between strokes. Forget cross-court shots and boasts. Just practise hitting the ball. When you can hit straight up and down in an orthodox fashion and with good timing you have gone a very long way in developing your stroke play.

Having mastered length shots—but not before—start practising drop shots. Be sure to mix hard hitting shots with the drop shots so you do not get into the habit of "poking" your drop shots.

Practising at home is very important because you can do it at any time. Mentally it does not strain you in the same way as going to a squash court and playing a game. If you practise at home every day, you will get to the stage where you can walk on to a court and always hit the ball in the right way.

PRACTICE ROUTINES

These routines are designed to develop all aspects of your stroke play. Always hit the ball with your body facing the side wall. Use a full swing, except in close quarter situations where a modified swing would be more effective.

BACKHAND

1. The player commences the stroke with a full backswing. The knees are well bent and weight is moving on to the right foot. Maximum racket head speed must be developed as in a full drive.

2. The racket head drops a little below the ball and then comes up to the point of contact. The ball must be hit very hard and upwards to the back wall to produce a high rebound (although lower than in a lob).

3. The follow-through goes high. The ball returns over the right shoulder, hits the front wall high up and near the opposite side wall, and rebounds close enough to the side wall and far enough down the court to restrict attacking shots by the opponent and leave the centre clear

BACK WALL CROSS-COURT BOAST

On your own

1. Hit length shots up and down the wall with a full but easy swing. The ball must land sufficiently behind the short line so that on the first bounce it ends at the back wall nick or the back wall so low that a return shot would be extremely difficult.

2. From a little behind the short line hit alternate hard shots (a little short) and drop shots, always starting with the racket upright.

3. At the front of the court, directly in front of the "T", play to the front wall on alternate sides so that the ball then hits the side wall and returns to you. Adjust your feet and keep the ball moving quickly. Vary this procedure with occasional drop shots to the nick from fast balls.

4. Vary routine 3 by hitting occasional high balls then hitting them into the nick on the volley.

With a friend

5. From the back of the service box hit a hard length shot down the wall, then hit a hard boast from the same position. Your friend returns it down the other wall and you repeat the one length shot, one boast routine.

6. Boast from the back of the court to your friend, who hits hard across court. You continue to boast back to him.

7. Boast from the back of the court to your friend, who attacks with any shot. As soon as you boast, go up to centre-court just behind the short line on the side of the centre line from which you boasted. Try to cut off his return as far up court as possible.

8. Your friend stands at the front of the court and you stand in the opposite angle of the "T". He hits the ball softly against the front wall, then hits any form of attacking shot as it bounces back. You must watch the ball and his racket, get to the ball quickly and attack if possible, preferably by volley.

9. Your friend serves and you must return the service deep and safely. Never let the service die—attack it every time.

10. Hit loose balls to one another to practice nick or drop shots.

11. Your friend hits a hard, low cross-court shot from deep in court. You must stand with your feet at 45 degrees to the side wall. Watch his stroke and turn with your feet and hips to cut it off at the short line with a drop shot into the near corner of the court.

World champion Geoff Hunt, who at 18 became the youngest player to ever win an Australian squash championship.

THE BASIC GAME

Squash rallies are not won easily or quickly. You must make your opponent run continually and work him out of position before you can hit a winner. The basic game, which opens the way to hitting a winner, keeps your opponent running continuously and is a very important part of your strategy.

The fundamental principles of the basic game in squash are to:

1. Take the centre of the court and make your opponent play from one of the four corners. Always play the shot that achieves this.
2. Be sure you can reach the centre prior to your opponent reaching the ball.
3. Make your shot apply maximum pressure on your opponent.
4. Never hit a shot that finishes in the middle of the court.
5. Use a lofted serve that hits the side wall, occasionally varying this with a fast serve.
6. Return your opponent's service deep down the side wall.
7. Make your opponent travel the maximum distance.
8. Make your basic shot down the wall furthest from your opponent.
9. Never hit across court unless you can pass your opponent.
10. Use boasts and drop shots basically to move your opponent out of position.
11. Use drop shots, boasts and nick shots only when you can regain the centre of the court quickly.
12. Always use good length.
13. Lob when in trouble.
14. Try not to be forced to boast out of back corners.
15. Eliminate "fancy" shots.
16. Get pace and length through good timing.

THE BASIC THEORY

If you have ever watched evenly matched top players playing one another you have probably noticed that they tend to share the centre of the court, the striker being away from the centre and the other awaiting his turn in the centre. However, if you watch an inexperienced player playing a top player you'll find that he covers a terrific amount of court while the expert monopolises the centre. Obviously the execution of strokes accounts for a good deal of the difference in standard, but there are two more important reasons why the inexperienced player gets such a trouncing. Firstly, he never gets a chance as the expert does to hit the ball from the centre of the court because his opponent's shots do not finish there, and secondly, he does not share the centre of the court because he does not play his opponent away from it.

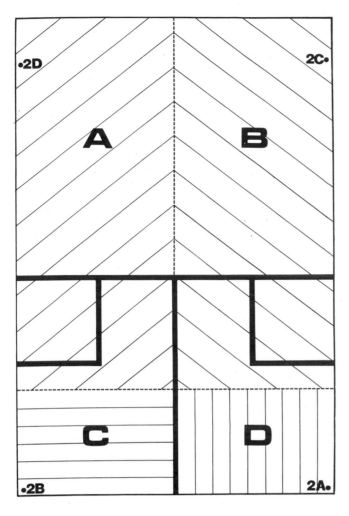

The Basic Game:

	A		2A
If your opponent is	B	your shot should	2B
in the area marked	C	finish at point	2C
	D		2D

The boundaries between the four areas in this diagram apply to a game against a fast, fresh opponent. The forward boundaries of areas C and D will not remain constant for all opponents or for all stages of a match, and you must alter them according to your own judgment. If, for example, your opponent is naturally slow or becomes tired, the forward boundary lines of these areas should be moved forward as you see fit.

The most important axiom of squash is: play your shot to take your opponent away from the centre to one of the four corners of the court and immediately take your position a metre behind the "T" so you are ready to pounce on any return he may make. When you have a choice of shots, always play the one that leaves you with the centre court position.

You may stand further forward if your opponent's shots lack severity or if you feel sure you can volley his return. Otherwise it is dangerous to move on to or past the short line before you know where he is hitting the ball.

The diagram (at left) shows the pattern to follow in playing a basic game. Learn it thoroughly because without it you will never master squash strategy. If your opponent is in a certain position on the court you must know exactly where your basic shot must finish. This, and an ability to take the centre of the court, are the primary approaches to tiring your opponent and paving the way to winners.

Think of the basic game as a forcing game that moves your opponent about at a fast pace and keeps him deep in the court unless you take him up court with a long boast or a medium paced drop shot. If you develop this basic game your opponent can only attack from deep in the court, which is always difficult.

PRESSURE

Your basic game must seek both to put your opponent under pressure and to relieve you of pressure by maintaining easy access to the centre. Try to make him run the maximum distance in the minimum time, provided this does not put you under comparable pressure to regain the centre before he hits the ball.

If you are in one of the four corners, be careful that the pace and placement of your shot are not such that your opponent can cut it off and play it before you can regain the centre. Otherwise it's likely that the pace of your own shot will be used against you!

Nevertheless, you should always be seeking to improve the pace and accuracy of your basic shots to make your opponent move faster and work harder than you do.

THE DANGER AREA

Never hit a shot that enables your opponent to take the ball in the "danger area" shown on the diagram (above right). Against any player of reasonable calibre this spells trouble.

THE SERVICE AND RETURN SHOT

Your standard serve should be a lofted serve that strikes the side wall towards the back of the opposite service box, just beyond the height of the extended racket of your opponent. He must not be able to volley your serve before it hits the side wall and you must make him either take it off the wall on the volley or wait until it bounces and take it near the

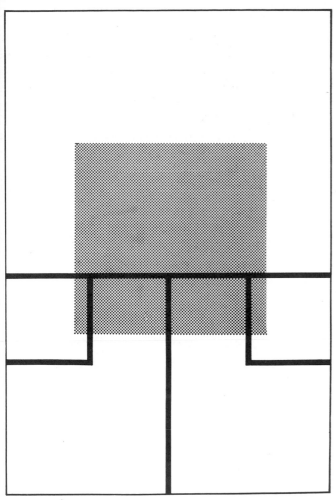

The Danger Area: Keep your shots out of the shaded area of the court shown on this diagram.

back wall. An intelligently directed fast service can be used as a variation.

Return of service should force your opponent to play his next shot as close as possible to one of the back corners or at least on a side wall near the back of the court. If possible volley your own return of service before the ball hits the side wall, otherwise take it on the volley after it hits the side wall; don't allow it to bounce unless you are sure you can hit an attacking shot off the rebound.

The basic return of service is a length shot down the side wall, which your opponent cannot cut off without leaving the centre of the court. Do not drive across court unless your opponent has moved out of position to attempt to cut off a shot down the wall.

THE DEEP GAME

As your basic game must always make your opponent travel the maximum distance in the minimum time which allows you to regain the centre, the predominant shot in this game is down the wall, the full length of the court, on the opposite side to your opponent. If he is on your left, hit the ball down the forehand wall; if he is on your right, hit it down the backhand wall. This stroke not only makes your opponent run the greatest distance possible, but it leaves you in the centre of the court ready to attack and him at the back of the court.

Hit across court only when you can hit the ball past your opponent and out of his reach. It must be hit so that it returns deep to make him come back after it. When you are at the back of the court you can only do this if he is a little out of position, but you will often get the opportunity from the front of the court. Wherever you are, do not simply hit the ball back across the court to your opponent every time he hits it to you. If he hits the ball across to you, hit it deep down the wall furthest away from him and then you can take control of the court.

THE SHORT GAME

Another essential part of your basic game is to move your opponent up and down the court. At this stage it is important to understand that boasts and drop shots are basically a variation added to a length game to move your opponent out of position and weaken him; and you should not build up a game based on these being the winning shots. You will, of course, win points outright from them, but if they become your "pet" shots you will be in a lot of bother when you play a good fast player with an understanding of squash strategy. However, used properly they will make a great difference to your game.

To use boasts and drop shots as part of your basic game you must keep your opponent deep in the court with your length game, otherwise they are of no advantage to you at all and will in fact give him the opportunity to attack. Keep your opponent back with length shots and use a boast or a drop shot primarily from back in the court to move him up the court out of position so you can force a weak return, cut it off and force him back again with an attacking length shot which could well be a winner.

There is a very true saying that your drop shots are as good as your length shots.

The decision as to whether either a boast or a drop shot should be used in a particular situation will depend largely on your accuracy with each shot, but you must also take into account the position of the ball when hit and where you desire it to finish. The following rules are useful:

1. When you want the ball to finish near the opposite front corner use a boast if the ball is hit near the wall or either shot if the ball is well clear

Hand-out (right) volleys his opponent's serve before it hits the side wall or, if that is not possible, after it hits the side wall — unless he is sure that he can hit an attacking shot off the rebound. Hand-out (below) retreats to take an accurate semi-lob serve on the bounce and will find himself constantly on the defensive from his first shot.

YES

NO

of the wall. If you are hitting the ball from very close to the front wall a drop shot will travel right across the court, while a delicate boast (angle shot) will not. The greatest advantage of this shot hit near the wall is that it can be hit with an apparent full swing and therefore keep your opponent covering a length shot.

2. When you want the ball to finish near the front corner nearest to you, use a drop shot.

Remember, you can not build a good game entirely around boasts and drop shots. They are to be used only in addition to your basic deep length game, which is the most important part of your strategy. The majority of winners in good squash come from length shots.

When you do a boast or drop shot be sure you can command the centre of the court before your opponent returns the ball; there's no point using one of these strokes if it leaves you out of position in taking his return. The ideal situation for playing a drop shot or boast is when the ball comes to you quickly and you know that your opponent is out of position and behind you.

LENGTH

The previous chapter dealt with length in terms of shots driven deep in the court. At this point it is essential to understand this subject in its full context as it is paramount in forcing your opponent to make his return from one of the four corners.

When the court is "open" in a certain sector your basic shot should take your opponent to the furthermost point of that sector. The test of good length for any shot—forceful drive, boast, nick shot, drop shot, reverse angle or lob—is whether or not it forces your opponent to attempt to make his return at (or beats him to) this furthermost point. (This point, of course, must be at or near a wall and is generally in one of the four corners.)

The whole art of basic squash centres around taking your opponent at maximum pace to the furthermost "open" point, leaving you in complete control in the centre. If you allow your shots to bounce off any wall and be retrieved you have lost a valuable advantage. Never hit short length or loose shots that can be cut off around the centre-court,

The opponent's shot has taken the player at full stretch to the front wall and she is unable to hit an attacking shot clear of her opponent. The player (right) lobs diagonally across court to give herself ample time to regain the centre-court position. The player (below) tries to hit her way out of this position and in doing so gives her opponent the opportunity to volley a winner.

YES

NO

especially near the short-line (i.e. in the "danger area"). If you think of the four corners and good length, you are well on the way to success.

THE LOB

The subject of lobbing (also known as tossing) concerns the basic game in that it enables you to regain the centre of the court if you are out of position at the front of the court. Regard the lob as a "must" if you can not do an attacking shot from the

front of the court. Lob high and diagonally across to the opposite back corner, then quickly resume your position and balance in the centre of the court. Attacking with a lob is dealt with in the next chapter.

DEFENSIVE RETRIEVING FROM BACK CORNERS

If you are forced to retrieve a ball defensively from a back corner of the court your shot will depend on the position of your opponent. Assuming he is well positioned and waiting to attack any defensive return, your priorities should be:

1. Turn your back to the front wall and with your forearm, wrist and hand hit the ball high, slow and tight along the side wall to come right back to the back wall.
2. Play the ball on to the back wall, rebounding over your shoulder to the front wall near the diagonally opposite corner and hugging that side wall on its return, safely away from the front wall (if you are good enough to do this accurately).
3. Boast out of the corner. "Put your head into the corner" and make the stroke entirely with your arm (keep your body out of it), meeting the ball as early as possible. There may be times when you think it would pay to hit a boast high to give you time to recover and move up the court, but the difficulty here is that the ball will generally return to the danger area and you'll lose control again.

SUMMARY

Concentrate on your basic game and do not attempt "fancy" shots. You can only develop winners when you have this sound background.

Your basic game constitutes a great proportion of the number of shots you play and therefore must not require too much effort. You must get your length and pace by timing rather than by "muscle". If your shot is a purely defensive one to put your opponent at the back of the court, simply hit the ball higher above the tin so that it finishes back there without any undue effort. If you "bash" every ball you will tend to lose accuracy and wear yourself out in a long match.

Practice playing a sound basic game every time you walk on a court so it becomes second nature to you.

PRACTICE ROUTINE FOR CONTROLLING THE GAME FROM THE CENTRE OF THE COURT

The aim of this routine is:

1. To apply pressure and maintain control from the centre of the court, one metre behind the "T".
2. To keep your opponent deep in the court except when *you* take him forward.
3. To avoid being forced to boast defensively.
4. To place every shot with the intention that you must occupy the central position before your opponent makes his stroke.
5. To be well balanced at the centre in time to watch the ball and your opponent's swing, his racket-head going through the ball and the direction of the ball when hit.

The routine is played in two stages. Perfect the strokes and positional control of stage 1 before moving to stage 2.

Stage 1

(a) Your opponent must not be able to put his racket to the ball (except when taken forward to the front wall) unless he is behind the position you will take up behind the "T" and also near a side wall.

(b) Every time you are taken to the front of the court you must lob the ball high out of his reach so it dies in the diagonally opposite back corner.

(c) Your only shots apart from the lob will be:

   (i) Firmly hit length shots finishing in one of the back corners. They should constitute seven out of every 10 shots hit and should always be to the open court, i.e. the side of the court opposite to where your opponent is placed. Generally you will be hitting down the wall. Make sure any cross-court drive can not be cut off but forces your opponent to retreat.

   (ii) Slow, high shots that cling to the side wall if you need time to go back to the centre.

   (iii) From deep in the court: attacking boasts at the same pace as length shots but only at times when you could firmly hit direct to the front wall if you wanted to.

   (iv) From or behind the short line when your opponent is behind you: a drop shot to the corner diagonally opposite that from which your opponent hit his shot, if practicable. Otherwise, a drop shot to the other front corner, into the nick or hugging the wall.

   (v) From within 60cm (24in) in front of or behind the short line and approximately level with the lengthwise service line: a full or three-quarter pace shot to the nick near the front wall on the opposite side of the court, hit from chest height or above.

   (vi) From deep in the court: a reverse boast as an occasional variation.

   (vii) From deep in the court when it appears you can not hit the ball direct to the front wall (i.e. your opponent hopes to force you to boast): your first aim should be to return the ball down the side wall if at all possible.

FOREHAND YES

NO

BACKHAND YES

NO

The player is forced as a last resort to boast the ball out of the back corner on to the side wall. She turns her back almost towards the front wall (left) so she can make her vertical backswing freely, without hitting the back wall. Her follow-through (centre) is clear of the side wall and the racket head will finish over her shoulder. Throughout the stroke she has kept her head steady and facing the corner. Her body has not moved and the shot has been made with her arm alone. The player (right) attempts the same shot with her back almost facing the back wall. She starts in a cramped position and as the ball is behind her she will have to step back even though this will further restrict her movements. Inevitably she must turn her body forward to try to hit the ball and has little chance of succeeding.

Dick Carter, twice runner-up in world championships, moves in to drive the ball from well in front of his front foot. A master of the classic basic game, he is noted for his ability to keep the game tight and tough.

Stand with your back to the front wall and hit the ball high, slow and tight to the side wall to come right back to the back wall. If you can't do this, play the ball on to the back wall, rebounding over your shoulder to the front wall near the diagonally opposite corner and returning close to the side wall as deep as possible.

Notes:

• Aim at controlling the game from the centre and forcing your opponent to hit from one of the four corners of the court.

• Play all your shots (except lobs) with a full swing, or in the case of a drop shot with an apparent full swing (start with racket head vertical).

• Take advantage of this practice to perfect your shots under (c) (vi) and (vii) which although seldom used in match play can be most effective in certain circumstances.

Stage 2

The restriction under (b) no longer applies. You may attack with any shot provided your opponent has to retreat to get it, but otherwise you must lob.

MATCH PLAY

Once you have mastered court movement, stroke play and the basic game, you are ready to learn the all-important subject of match play.

To be a champion in match play you must:

1. Hit the ball correctly so you are always in a position to hit an attacking shot or the necessary defensive shot to or from anywhere on the court.

2. Never take your eyes off the ball and show pace between the two most important positions—when your opponent is hitting the ball and when you are hitting the ball. Be balanced when in these positions and recover quickly to the centre after hitting the ball.

3. Incorporate these qualities in a perfect basic game designed to run your opponent about as much as possible while you command the game from the centre of the court.

These are the weapons you must have within your control before you commence the climb to the top in match play.

Let us study the techniques of the world's top professionals:

1. Their stroke play is correct and they can play any stroke with ease.

2. They disguise their shots because their backswings are always the same and they can apply pressure in the last stages of their swings.

3. The pace of their shots comes from perfect timing with minimum effort.

4. They are always perfectly balanced and their footwork and mobility are outstanding.

5. Every shot they hit makes the opponent run maximum distance leaving them in command of the court; in other words, they have perfect basic games combined with consistent accuracy.

6. They are fit and can keep on their toes throughout a hard match.

7. Their match strategy is very sound.

Top professionals are where they are simply because they are proficient in applying these fundamentals. They do not do anything which is new to others. They do what others know is correct but they do it better than others can.

To be a champion you too must become an expert at all aspects of your basic game.

The fundamental principles of correct match play in squash are:

1. Play a "pressurised" basic game by:
   (a) getting to the ball early through watching your opponent play his stroke;
   (b) hitting the ball deliberately to searching length; and
   (c) maintaining control and never ceasing trying to attack.

2. Make yourself capable of playing tighter and being physically tougher than your opponents.

3. Winners are always preceded by getting your opponent out of position or off balance.

4. Play your basic shot if your opponent is standing still.

5. When your opponent is hurrying to regain his position alternate between your basic shot and a shot designed to "wrong foot" him.

6. A delayed shot can help to "wrong foot' an opponent.

7. In match play:
   (a) be calm, never get excited;
   (b) keep your eye on the ball;
   (c) play a "pressurised" basic game and keep the ball deep; and
   (d) hit your opponent's weak return before he can regain position.

8. The first shot of a rally can be vital.

9. Never turn on the back wall to take service.

10. Concentrate on length, particularly early in the match.

11. Restrict short shots early in the match and always precede them with many length shots.

12. Later in the game, run your opponent up and down the court more.

13. Always be well positioned and balanced ready to volley, but don't throw yourself off balance to do it.

14. Vary shots hit from near the front wall; lob if in difficulty.

15. Always make your opponent feel the necessity to cover your basic game.

16. Boast from time to time from the back of the court in tight rallies to upset your opponent's rhythm and take him away from the centre.

17. A long drop shot is a quick and valuable attacking shot off a loose shot.

18. Never allow your shot to end in the centre of the court.

19. Don't be afraid to do any form of attacking shot if you know you can take the centre of the court before your opponent hits his return.

20. Although concentration on the ball is your first priority, always try to know where your opponent is.

21. Vary the pace of your shots.

22. Don't waste energy.

23. Maintain your balance.

24. Don't trail your racket head.

25. Be patient in rallies.

26. Don't have "pet" shots.

27. Eradicate any weakness which can be attacked.

28. Always remember:
    (a) your drop shot is as good as your length shot; and
    (b) your "wrong-footer" is as good as your basic game.

29. Learn how to read the game (see page 92).

A "PRESSURISED" BASIC GAME

Many players enter a squash game with the idea that they must try to hit a winner off the first ball they think they can handle. Nothing could be more wrong. The first thought should be to play a good basic game which will present opportunities for winners; the second thought should be to seize such an opportunity and attempt a winner; and the third thought should be that a good opponent is quite likely to retrieve an attempted winner, so balance and position must be maintained in anticipation of the rally continuing.

You should approach match play with the idea of playing a "pressurised" basic game. Your fundamental basic game already enables you to take control and run your opponent about. If you put pressure into it too, you put pressure on to him from a sound tactical position. This is all part of the strategy needed for success in most competitive sports. If a boxer throws wild punches and ignores the basic principles which enable him to attack from a position fundamentally safe from attack by his opponent, he will be knocked out very quickly. The same principle applies to squash. If you play a match wildly, forgetting your basic game, you will soon find yourself in a physically helpless position against any astute opponent.

You must therefore develop a "pressurised" basic game which enables you to attack but is also fundamentally safe against attack from your opponent. Always playing the shot which leaves you in control of the court will in itself go a long way towards achieving this, but the main ways of increasing pressure are:

1. Get to the ball early by watching both the ball and your opponent when he is striking it.

2. When you get to the ball early hit a full stroke; never rush your shot. You need clean, searching, good length shots hit hard enough to make your opponent work hard if he is to retrieve them.

3. Always maintain control and never cease trying to attack.

If you work on these points you will automatically put pressure into your game.

TIGHT AND TOUGH

The standard of your fitness and the pressure of your basic game must be of such a high standard that you can confidently go into a match saying "I'm going to make it tight and tough and the longer the rallies the better". You must train and practise so assiduously

The Australian amateur team of 1962-3, which first established Australia as a world squash power. The players are (left to right): Owen Parmenter, Doug Stephenson, Ken Binns, John Cheadle, Ken Hiscoe and Dick Carter.

that you are confident you can do this and not have it done to you.

Heather McKay is seldom spectacular in the first game, but she occupies the centre and makes it so tight and tough on her opponents that most are reduced almost to struggling average players before the second game is far advanced—or they try risky shots early against tight placements and fall into error.

When you are faced with an opponent who is tighter and tougher than you are, slow down your shots to give yourself more time to return to the centre and use all your guile to upset his rhythm.

WINNERS

How do you hit winners in a tight game of long rallies? To answer this question you must take into account two important points. First, you can not, without a good deal of luck, hit a winner against your opponent when he is well-balanced in the centre-court position. Secondly, your winners must

be preceded by tactical manoeuvres and searching stroke play designed to put your opponent out of position or off balance.

By sheer pace in moving to the ball and making accurate and severe shots you can gradually get the edge on your opponent during a basic game rally and hit an outright winner that he cannot reach. If you are getting to the ball early and your opponent is getting to the ball late it is only a matter of time before a sound basic game will overwhelm him. By consistently playing a searching basic game instead of trying risky winning shots you tighten up the game on your opponent and make him run in seemingly endless rallies. If you are the fitter of the two this must lead to ultimate success because once he slows down and is late to the ball you have him.

You should consider a basic attacking shot as one hit to the corner farthest from your opponent so he must hurry to cover it. You can also "wrong foot" him when he is running away from a corner or wall in a belated attempt to cover the basic shot by hitting the ball so it finishes as near as possible to the corner or position he has left or crosses his line of flight with such effect that he can not retrieve it without propping, turning and using considerable effort and pace.

In seeking winners in match play it is sound practice to play a searching basic shot if your opponent is standing still, regardless of whether he's in a good or a hopeless position. If, however, you are hitting the ball when he is still hurrying to regain his position, alternate between basic shots and shots designed to "wrong foot" him. The uncertainty created in his mind will give you greater scope for a winning shot.

You can "wrong foot" an opponent who is coming back from the front of the court by using a boast or a drop shot, or in certain cases by hitting across his line of flight to finish in the back corner on the side from which he hit.

Likewise, you can "wrong foot" an opponent who is racing to the front of the court by hitting a length shot. If he has returned weakly from a back corner and is racing to get forward, you can "wrong foot" him by hitting to the other back corner or to the one he has left.

These tactics are possible only if you are perfect in your basic game and apply it with pressure. Provided you are doing this throughout you will find ample opportunity to make your opponent twist and turn to chase shots hit against his line of flight. Remember, these shots may not always be winners but they inevitably take steam out of him.

Keep your opponent moving by applying pressure so that sooner or later you can hit a winner. If you get him to mentally cover your basic shot you'll have him racing to cover it, then you'll have a chance to hit a shot in the opposite direction. The reason two good players can play a cross-court game to one another as a variation is that each knows he must cover the other's down-the-wall shots and cannot risk waiting out of position for a cross-court shot. In other words each player has felt the pressure of the other's basic game, and mentally must cover the shots arising from it. They often attempt to tire one another by switching play across court, forcing the opponent to first cover the down-the-wall shot then go back to the cross-court shot.

However, a word of warning. Many players have a tendency to learn the correct basic game and start to apply it in matches, then become elated when an occasional change of direction produces winners, as of course it should. Encouraged by this, they more frequently change the direction of their shots to across the court towards their opponent and eventually this becomes their basic game. Instead of hitting the ball away from their opponents to apply pressure, they become so keen on what they consider is the winning shot that they start hitting the ball back to them! Obviously, they lose control.

This also happens when players repeatedly play boasts or drop shots without first applying pressure with length shots to stop their opponent from moving forward early.

Always remember to induce your opponent to move by making him try to cover your basic game. If you have taken him to the front of the court, for instance, he must feel that you are going to cut off his return and put it down the opposite side wall. This forces him, as soon as he's hit the ball, to return as quickly as possible to the centre of the court to cover that shot or even race directly to the opposite wall. If you can get to the ball early enough—while he is still moving—you have him.

The only way to "wrong foot" an opponent is to get in quickly enough to catch him leaving his previous position and moving to the position which he intends to take up. You can not "wrong foot" an opponent when he is balanced properly and in position waiting for your shot. Too many people hit a cross-court shot or a boast to an opponent who is poised and ready for the ball. The whole essence of variation of play from a basic game is that it must be applied only when your opponent is moving.

In looking for winners, remember that your drop shot is as good as your length shot, and your "wrong footer" is as good as your basic game.

THE DELAYED SHOT

It is not easy to "wrong foot" an opponent who is a good tactical player. He will know that you are looking for an opportunity to do so and when out of position will keep himself well-balanced, whether moving or not, until he is sure he knows where you are going to hit the ball.

Here, the perfect stroke play you have learned enables you still to have a chance to force a winner.

Your opponent knows he should not move until he sees where you are going to hit the ball and, as your backswing is the same for all shots, he is aware that he will have to start late and from a bad position to cover a searching shot, which he knows you can hit by going out after the ball and timing it well. Therefore his plan will be to improve his position slowly with well-balanced footwork while you are preparing to strike the ball, to be steady during your stroke, to delay movement as long as possible in the hope of seeing what shot you are hitting, and to then make an all-out attempt to get to the ball.

As you are a good strokemaker, you place your

feet and make your backswing in a manner which your opponent knows applies to any shot you care to hit. Since the stroke you intend to play will not be evident until late in your forward movement, you know your opponent cannot move quickly until then and must therefore throw himself off balance the moment he makes his decision.

As you normally hit the ball in front of your feet, you can delay your shot a fraction of a second and still hit it well. In so doing you will "wrong foot" even an experienced opponent because provided your action has not given him a clue to other intentions there will come a point when he must move to cover the obvious basic shot. He must put everything into his movement and if you can then play a shot against his obvious line of flight you will create and clinch a winning position.

In delaying your shot you have not gone so far forward for the ball and as a result it is generally closer to the floor than usual when hit. You will find that a drive, boast or drop shot can be conveniently played in this position with sufficient effect to capitalise on the position created.

This manoeuvre is another feature of squash tactics. The basic shots, and probably most shots designed to "wrong foot" your opponent, are played very early, while a valuable variation against a top-class opponent is a delayed shot to make him move and be off-balance when the ball is ultimately hit against his line of flight.

An interesting but difficult to accomplish example of this is Roshan Khan's delayed cross-court drop shot played from the forecourt. He goes through the action of playing a drop shot to the near corner but, as his opponent moves quickly towards that corner, delays his shot and from very low down does a delicate cross-court drop shot which finishes near the opposite wall.

Surprisingly, against a fast and determined opponent, this delayed shot can be adapted to an early shot. If you have made your opponent boast defensively out of the back corner and he knows you are waiting to drop the ball short in the diagonally opposite front corner, he will almost certainly run full speed towards that corner. If you set yourself for a drop shot in this corner and, without changing your stance, bring the racket early and quickly across to meet the ball in front of your body (forehand) or still further across (backhand) you can hit the ball just over the tin at half pace to be well out of his reach and finish before it reaches the other side wall in front of the short line. The sheer speed at which your opponent must move to cover the near wall drop shot gives this variation the effect of a delayed shot.

THE MENTAL APPROACH

Before you go on the court there are four things you must have in mind:
1. You must be calm no matter what happens. If you get excited on a squash court you will ruin your game. You will rush your strokes and mis-time, and the pace of the game will make you even more irrational. You have to move quickly but you must do it calmly. No matter what happens, never get excited or allow anything to upset you. Ignore any temperamental behaviour from your opponent.
2. You must keep your eye on the ball wherever it goes and watch it right on to your racket. If you do that all your training will be worthwhile. If you do not, you will be late to the ball and you may also hit strokes like a beginner. You simply must keep your eye on the ball to benefit from all the time you have spent learning to move early and play your strokes soundly.
3. You must play a pressurised basic game and keep the ball deep until you want to take your opponent forward.
4. You are trying to make your opponent make a weak return, and when he does you must hit it before he can regain his position.

THE FIRST SHOTS

The first shot of a rally can very often determine its outcome.

I have already stressed the importance of always taking the centre of the court. If your first shot is loose, the pressure is on you and you will have trouble getting there. So always be sure that your first shot is accurate and searching.

You must not let your opponent volley your service before it hits the side wall because he would have the chance to attack on the first ball and make you defend. Your service must be accurate and he must be forced back. If you find he is too successful in taking the ball off the wall and attacking from that position, vary the pace a little to upset his timing. It is difficult to accurately time a ball off the wall and he may have reached the stage of mastering a return of your particular service. Alternatively, serve a fast ball straight at him to shake him up.

In nearly all cases you should return your opponent's service deep down the wall with accuracy and pace. If he is out of position and on your side of the centre, your basic shots are a boast if he is deep in the court and a cross-court length shot if he is forward in the court.

YES

The striker (above) has correctly assessed that his opponent's service will bounce well across the court and out from the back wall. With his opponent forced away from the centre, he attacks it from a good position. The striker (right) has incorrectly assessed his opponent's service and failed to volley it before it dies in the back corner. He now has little hope of retrieving it.

NO

An important point: if your opponent serves hard and deep against the side wall and the ball goes across and bounces off the back wall there are two possible ways of attacking it, but there is only one right way. New squash players often follow the ball and turn completely around before hitting it, thinking that is the clever way to do it. It is in fact both a dangerous way and the wrong way to do it. If the ball bounces across the court you should move backwards across the court and hit it on the forehand if it was originally on your forehand, or on the backhand if it was on your backhand. As you walk back, your opponent has to walk back also. If he is anywhere near the back of the court he has to get well out of your way because of your follow-through. The further the ball goes across the court the better because if you back across the court and hit it at the last moment you will have almost the whole court to hit into. If you turn around you will not force your opponent back so far and you will not be able to hit the ball so well. Furthermore, turning around is extremely dangerous and unfair to your opponent.

ATTACK WITH LENGTH

Now let's deal with general play. You start the match with the object of playing a "pressurised" basic game. The portion of the basic game you should concentrate on early in the match is the length basic game which aims at keeping your opponent back rather than moving him up and down the court. If you try a boast or a drop shot while your opponent is fresh he can get to it too quickly and may attack and hit a winner. So in the early stages you must hit searching length shots.

In the first rallies you should hit 6-10 length shots in a row to move your opponent's centre of operations back from the central position. The shot which takes him forward should be a boast or a drop shot played when he is deep in the court. Your previous length shots ensure that he does not anticipate your shot and use early pace to kill the ball.

So remember, early in a match go for length and do not overdo moving your opponent up to the front of the court—and on no account move him up without paving the way with length shots.

After the initial rallies move him forward more often, with say four length shots to one short shot for about 10 minutes. As you are still paving the way by mainly hitting length shots you are continuing to move him up and down the court giving him no opportunity to attack your short shots. These are

extremely good tactics because by moving him around so much you are taking the edge of his pace.

When the pace of the match has steadied a little the length to short shot ratio can be reduced to 3:1 and later to 2:1, but keep your opponent deep when you are not taking him forward. Of course, there will be occasions when the shortcomings of an opponent will dictate an earlier extensive use of the short game, but be very sure of this before you act.

Above all, your game should be based on applying pace and length to the ball with the *periodic* variation of taking the pace and length off the ball. To commence a match with the thought that the game is based on mainly taking the pace off the ball with short shots can be disastrous.

FORECOURT SHOTS

If you take your opponent forward make him stretch for the ball and hit across court, cut off his return early, and send the ball down the opposite side wall so he must run the maximum distance. When he becomes used to this basic shot and knows he must cover it, you can switch to a length shot across court and catch him on the wrong foot as he comes back from the front of the court. However, he must anticipate that you will hit the correct basic shot if he is out of position before you swing a shot across court to "wrong foot" him.

If you have taken your opponent forward with a boast or drop shot and find you can volley his return without serious body effort, step in quickly and do so. Always position yourself in the angle of the "T" on the side of the court opposite your opponent to give yourself the best chance of doing this.

The more pressure you can put on an opponent by taking the ball soon after he hits it, the better. However, do not continually throw yourself off balance to make volleys or you will seriously weaken yourself. Never throw your body to reach a volley unless you are sure of hitting a winner. If you can move quickly across court and volley, do so. But if you'd have to lunge and almost throw yourself off your feet, don't try. If your opponent is doing that against you, don't worry. Keep your basic game going and he will ultimately weaken, even though he might be dangerous early in the match. In any event he will be slow to recover after hitting a volley when off balance and you can generally play your return shot against his temporary unbalance.

Now, what do you do if you are taken to the front of the court yourself? The answer depends on how early you get to the ball and on where your opponent is placed on the court.

Twice runner-up in world championships, Australian Dick Carter follows through after making a chest-high volley down the wall from deep in the forehand court.

Australia's first official women's team to tour Great Britain (1967). In a close tussle with the previously unbeaten British team, the Australian girls won the series, 2-1. The players are (left to right): Marion Hawcroft, Marlene Tierney, Heather McKay, Robin Kennedy and Barbara Baxter.

It is perfectly safe to hit an attacking shot down the wall if your opponent is well positioned in the centre of the court waiting for your return. He will be sent back enabling you to take the centre. If, however, you get to the ball early and before he is properly positioned, you can take it well ahead of your feet, hitting forcefully and deep across court so it passes him and does not come off the side wall. This shot is very difficult for your opponent to return unless he is properly balanced in the centre of the court. A variation, should he anticipate this shot and stand wide, is to pull the ball further across so it hits the side wall near the floor on the full and behind him, and on the bounce swings behind him against his line of movement.

If there is any doubt about where your opponent is, and you are there early enough to hit an attacking shot, hit down the wall. But if you are there late, and stretching, and you are not sufficiently certain of your opponent's position or your ability to hit the stroke to enable you to pass him, always lob high over him, trying to make the ball die in the diagonally opposite corner. On the way down, this shot should hit the side wall, very close to the back

wall. With practice it can be not only a defensive shot, but a winning shot. As your opponent is well up the court you can confidently concentrate on making the ball die in the corner, knowing he can not volley it. Once it gets there, it can easily be a winner. So, if you are stretching and near the front wall lob high to the diagonally opposite corner; if you get there late you may have to lob along the wall.

If your opponent stands deep and out of position after sending you forward, a drop shot to the near corner can be an outright winner. The ultimate in skill is to prepare to play this shot so your opponent rushes in to get it, but to switch to a cross-court drop shot or wide low shot that passes him. A switch to a delicate "boast drop shot" can also be effective if he rushes in early to play his shot.

Above all, should your opponent consistently take you to the front wall do not always make the same shot. That is the worst thing you could do. He would learn very quickly and be there waiting to hit a winner, knowing you are hopelessly out of position. Even when he commands the game you must keep him wondering and not allow him to move early to your shot.

DOWN THE WALL

The main aim is to play a good length game and hit shots which go the full length of the court and make your opponent hit the ball from a position that enables you to command the court.

In a match between two good players most length shots are hit down the wall one after the other. If you build up your game on attack solely from the front of the court your opponent will never let you get there and you won't have any attack. You must therefore build your game on attack from anywhere.

The most difficult shot to attack from is a length shot down the wall. If you can get your racket on to it cleanly enough, hit it hard down the wall. But sometimes your opponent is better positioned than you are and therefore hitting the ball more accurately and more severely, so you cannot hit the ball down the wall other than defensively. How can you vary your game to stop him from hopping in quickly every time you hit and hitting his shot down the side wall, thereby keeping you back behind him? If his return is always tight the answer is to boast from the back of the court off a low ball. Surprisingly few people have learned this shot properly and can do it with consistent accuracy. However to my mind it should be part of your basic game, and you should be able to hit it as accurately, consistently and with the same backswing as you hit a shot down the wall. If you can do this shot your opponent cannot leave the centre of the court as he must cover a shot to the diagonally opposite corner. The moment he moves back out of position, you can attack by taking him up to the front wall.

In a deep game a long drop shot played from behind the opponent to either corner is a valuable variation and frequently catches him on his heels, but it can only be played off a ball which is well clear of the side wall.

If your opponent is cutting off your down-the-wall shots at the short line and is forward ready to pounce on any short shot, a hard, low cross-court shot is very effective as it will be difficult for him to see and cut off quickly.

CROSS-COURT PLAY

As mentioned earlier in this chapter play can be switched across court when you are sufficiently early to the ball to catch your opponent out of position. This can be very effective if you command the front of the court and hit accurately to the corners. Once you have started him running from side to side, you can tire him very easily by making him retrace his steps to play his shot. To do this you must get to the ball early and always catch him when he is moving away from the corner.

If these tactics are being used against you the most effective counter is a defensive shot deep down the wall or, if your opponent is covering this shot too closely, a deep cross-court shot or boast according to his position. However, you should generally try for the slow, high, deep shot hugging the wall.

ACCURACY, POSITION AND OBSERVATION

At this point it is necessary to emphasise two important points about your basic game. Firstly, your shot must never end in the "danger area", and secondly, it must never enable your opponent to step in and make you rush to your next shot. Hitting a ball which ends in the centre of the court is, of course, a classic example of this but there are many others.

Suppose you find yourself in a difficult position at the back of the court and you have the choice of perhaps two shots, one defensive and the other a risky attack. Always play the defensive shot which enables you to regain the centre of the court. Never hit an attacking shot if there is a chance your opponent can cut it off quickly, because if he does you'll lose the opportunity of taking the centre of the court before he makes his return and therefore give him the chance of hitting a winner while you are still moving.

It is fundamental that you be ready and balanced at the centre of the court when your opponent hits his shot. You must also save your legs. Give yourself the opportunity of taking the centre of the court without rushing. Always adopt this outlook when you are in trouble and you will re-establish your position with a minimum of effort. A good maxim is: when in trouble always lob or, if hitting from back in the court, hit a high shot hugging the side wall.

You can hit any shot safely, including a drop shot or a boast, *provided you can get back to the centre of the court before your opponent hits his return.*

You must develop a tendency to move up and down the centre of the court in preparation for your final movement to the ball. Hold your head high while moving to have the best possible view of the action. This way you can see what your opponent does after hitting the ball without taking your eyes off the ball itself.

YES

To play a shot near the front corner of the backhand court the striker (above) has moved forward up the centre, then turned across to a comfortable position from the ball. As she has been able to sight the whole of one side of the court she can closely assess the likely position of her opponent. The striker (right) has taken a direct path to the ball and cannot sight any part of the court behind her. She therefore cannot assess the position of her opponent.

NO

VARIATION IN PACE

Variation in pace is an extremely important strategical weapon in squash.

A player easily accustoms himself to taking shots that always come at the same pace and improves his timing as the game progresses. Under these circumstances it is difficult to force errors in his stroking. But you can often do so by varying the pace of your shots—provided you conceal your intentions by using a consistent backswing for all shots, hard or soft.

If you get to the ball early and hit it with surprising pace you can force your opponent off balance and take the sting out of his shots, and if you pop in an occasional drop shot you can catch him on his heels. It is an interesting fact, also, that some hard hitters cannot handle a "nothing ball", i.e. one with loft but little pace. You should give such opponents a good proportion of these, carefully placed so they can not be volleyed.

CONSERVATION OF ENERGY

Many Australian championship matches have been lost over recent years due to fatigue overcoming players who were regarded as extremely fit. The point is that in a squash match, fitness is relative only to the two players involved. No matter how fit you are you must conserve as much energy as you possibly can because your opponent is undoubtedly very fit too!

Common examples of lack of attention to conservation of energy are:

(a) *Attempting to hit nick shots from a bad strategical position.*
You cannot afford to do this as you will be caught out of position and have to tear from the front wall to the back wall to recover the return at a time when there is already extreme pressure in the game. The answer is to be sure before hitting the ball that your opponent is sufficiently out of position (or you are sufficiently in position) for you to finish or command the rally.

(b) *Not using the back wall to save the legs.*
Unfortunately too few people know how to do this shot. The ball is hit to the back wall to rebound diagonally across the court to the front wall near the side wall and come back along the side wall. With practice you can become extremely accurate at this shot and you will be surprised at how useful it can be. Kerim, in particular, showed us how to do this shot off a full-blooded drive from his opponent which

had, to all practical purposes, passed him. It is too good a defensive shot and too valuable in conserving energy for any top player to ignore. Hit the ball high to give yourself time to recover your position and make sure it finishes down the side wall and not near the centre of the court.

(c) *Lack of use of the lob as a defensive shot.*
Often a good short shot from your opponent has you stretching at full length, not able to recover quickly, while he is in position. Too many players try to hit their way out of such a position, but a good high lob to the opposite back corner would give them a chance to get back to the centre of the court and make the opponent, who was applying pressure in the rally, lose command. There is nothing more disconcerting to an opponent who feels he is about to hit a winner than to find that he is forced to the back wall while you take the centre of the court.

(d) *Bad use of attack from the corners.*
If you attack from any one of the four corners (front or back walls) you create the possibility that you may have to reach the diagonally opposite corner in very short time. Therefore you must do two things. Firstly, make sure your opponent cannot cut off your shot quickly, and secondly, return as quickly as possible to the central area. If you are not confident that your attacking shot will take him to one of the four corners, or perhaps feel a little tired, hit a lofted shot (perhaps a high slow shot down the wall) which will give you ample time to return to the centre before he makes his shot.

So, no matter how young and strong your legs are you still need to conserve them as much as you can, otherwise the final game may find you out.

BALANCE

Balance is an extremely important, though often underestimated, part of the tactical game. You have probably often seen someone who you know can hit a ball hard and accurately, lack sting in his shots or hit them too high. In top squash this is normally because his opponent has knocked him off balance by taking the ball early and hitting it with a full stroke so hard that he is surprised by the pace, put back on his heels and progressively loses sting and touch in his own stroke-making. The more his shots lose sting the easier and more effective his opponent's attack becomes.

You can guard against your opponent using this tactic on you, and possibly even be able to use it on him, by:

1. Watching your opponent hit the ball to get the earliest possible indication of his shot.

Champion Australian player Cam Nancarrow follows through after hitting a backhand smash to the left-hand front nick. He was well under the point of contact and sliced the ball heavily.

2. Always having your weight forward and striving to hit off the front foot.
3. Always approaching the ball with your back-swing well under way so the speed of the ball will not catch you unprepared and unable to hit your fall shot effectively.
4. Trying to keep your opponent under pressure.

DON'T TRAIL THE RACKET HEAD

A common mistake made by players when in command of the front of the court is to trail the racket head and consequently mis-hit a ball which comes to them quickly, simply because they cannot get the racket head to it in time. When in a position on the court where the ball may return to you quickly, always carry your racket head straight up. From this position you can hit almost any shot very quickly. As you move about the court carry your racket at approximately 90 degrees to your forearm and it will automatically come to vertical as you prepare for a shot.

PATIENCE AND CONCENTRATION

To be a champion you must have patience, total concentration and a willingness to work to develop openings. You must maintain control and wait for the opportunity to move your opponent a bit faster and step in for a winning shot. Self-discipline is essential. There is one thing of which you may be sure: squash will never become a game like tennis where a serve and volley can end so many rallies. Concentrate, and be patient!

"PET" SHOTS

The average tennis player has one or two pet shots and loves to manipulate his game so he can use them. It is quite usual—you see it even in high grade tennis. Similarly, most new squash players tend to develop their own pet shots. But if you want to do well in squash match play you must not do this. You are very close to your opponent in squash and he can recognise very quickly when you are going to do a pet shot. It is apparent in your make-up, the way you move and the way you position yourself. If he knows you are about to do a pet shot, he knows just where it will go and how hard you will hit it and he can easily hit a winner off it. You might like some shots better than others but do not make them apparent to your opponent or he will either capitalise on them or not give you a chance to do them.

In particular, be wary of the "forecourt reverse boast" or, perhaps more correctly, "forecourt reverse angle shot". This shot is hit when you are up at the front of the court in front of your opponent. You pull the ball across court to the side wall so it bounces to the front wall and comes across in front of you. In nearly all cases the swing of the racket, from the time it starts, makes it obvious to your opponent where the ball is going. Also, very few people do it without placing their feet in a position peculiar to that shot. It is so easy to pick—and can be so dangerous—that you should never include it in your basic game. It should be used only in isolated instances as a surprise shot, and even then it must be hit almost at your feet so it is impossible to tell until the last fraction of a second where the shot is going to be played. Your opponent must be deep in the court and expecting a shot to come there before you should even consider using a forecourt reverse boast.

A reverse boast played when both you and your opponent are at the back of the court is, however, a valuable occasional stroke provided you disguise it well because it finishes close to the front wall and away from your opponent.

OTHER POINTS TO WATCH

If you want to get to the top in squash you must learn to hit either winners or pressure shots off your opponents' tight shots. Some players, particularly because of the sensational impact of the nick shot, have wonderful scoring shots off loose balls but when pitted against someone who plays a tight and accurate game have little attack to their game. You must have a complete game and spend much of your time learning how to attack against accurate shots.

To become a champion at squash you have to play not twice but at least five times a week for a long period. Pre-war Australian champion Mervyn Weston, for example, played twice a day and seven days a week over a long period. Methods of training are dealt with in "Training and Nutrition" (see page 101).

It is impossible to cover all phases of match play in a book. Individual players will find that a match is better suited to them if it is played in a certain way and they will accordingly try to bring that about. In fact, countless possibilities present themselves. The theory of match play developed here, however, covers all the important aspects of top-grade squash. Stroke play embodying timing, accuracy, variation of pace and deception must be within the capability of every aspiring champion. He must have pace to and from the ball, and perfect balance both when hitting the ball himself and when watching his opponent hit it. He must have a sound basic game which enables him to keep his opponent running so he can regain the centre of the court after each shot.

It is vitally important to know these basic fundamentals early in your career if you want to be capable of tackling the championship arena later on. I feel sure that if you follow the advice offered in this book your own natural ability will be given every opportunity and you will not suffer later in your career because of early mistakes.

POLISHING YOUR GAME

The best way to build up your knowledge of match play and therefore bring your game to the highest possible standard is to combine hard practical experience with study. A balanced approach towards gaining this knowledge is:

1. Learn correct technique.
2. Persist in using this correct technique in match play until your game is lifted to higher competitive levels. Do not compromise if this does not seem to work early.
3. Learn to "read the game":
   (a) when you are sure your basic shots are good; and
   (b) when you may be at fault.

EXPERIENCE

Extensive match play experience against really good players is unquestionably the only way to remove the rough edges from your game. However match play experience is of limited value and can, indeed, be damaging unless:

1. You have previously, by practice and study, brought your game to the stage where you consistently use correct technique and carry it into match play with a determination to improve it under pressure. Do not discard it even if you have early losses.

2. You are playing against good, hard players who make it necessary for you to use correct strategy, movement and strokes to win.

Your first priority must be to develop correct technique. If you develop your game ignoring this technique you have little chance of reaching the top. Many players, for example, find they can win rallies in lower grades by using pet shots. Early success leads to improvising or copying further flashy shots or tactics. The deficiencies of pet shots and faulty court movement can be more than compensated for in lower grades by sheer athletic ability. But they will be a serious liability in higher competition. By that time they'll be so firmly entrenched that only years of heartbreaking "surgery" can remedy the situation.

To be successful you must develop gradually, strictly carrying into match play everything you have been taught in practice—court movement, watching the ball, stroke play and the basic game.

The most difficult and challenging part of your development is retaining confidence in your correct technique when under pressure of early match defeats by players with somewhat unorthodox styles. Despite technique limitations, many players reach a reasonably high standard of match play by sheer force of years of play against good players. But they will never reach the top.

These players use their own particular abilities well and with great consistency. Their match play experience is used intelligently to pick any particular weaknesses you may have and to exploit the fact that you have not yet "put your game together". You must have the courage to accept such defeats and rectify weaknesses until you have a complete match technique to lift you above such opponents.

Always honestly assess and admit the reasons for a defeat or any weaknesses evident in a win. Analyse your own performance, question your coach or experienced top players, and discuss the game with your opponent. Open discussion is invaluable and promotes confidence.

Unfortunately good match players are not made overnight and you must be patient.

READING THE GAME

Probably the most essential ingredient of experience is the ability to "read" what is happening in a match so you can recognise the opportunities presented and also any changes needed in your strategy or technique.

When your basic shots are good

Your basic attitude to the game should be to continually watch your opponent hitting his shots, get quickly to the ball, and accurately (and usually forcefully) play to the open court a shot designed to make him run maximum distance in minimum time, so you can wait patiently for a weak return or evidence that he is sufficiently out of position for you to hit a shot which could be a winner.

But what is the evidence that your opponent is out of position? This is an important aspect of the game and one that you should take particular care to learn. Very often what appears to be a complete failure of the basic theory and the prospect of loss of a match is really the evidence you are waiting for.

Let us take several examples to explain exactly what is meant by "reading the game".

(a) *You get to the ball more quickly than your opponent does, hit the ball more accurately to the open court, and return to the centre more quickly. He gets later and later to his shots.*

You can see you are playing a better basic game than he is, so you keep up the pressure until you finally hit a winner to the open court because he has not been able to regain the centre position soon enough.

(b) *Under a similar hypothesis, his inferior technique leads him to recover from one shot and move at full speed directly to cover the next obvious basic*

shot without going to the centre and being balanced to cover any shot.

He is covering your basic game and returning your shots, but your objective has been achieved! Your basic game has caused him to risk being out of position. The most obvious example of this is when you take your opponent to a front corner and he gambles on your hitting his return down the far wall and rushes directly to cover it. He presents you with the opportunity of hitting a winning return by hitting a deep cross-court shot across his line of flight or returning the ball to the corner he has just left.

(c) *You are occupying the centre of the court in front of your opponent and hitting deep and with pressure. Your opponent is getting to the ball comfortably and apparently using less energy than you are and you may feel he has mastered your game.*

Obviously he is remaining deep and making no attempt to return to the centre of the court after each shot to cover shots to all four corners. Your object is achieved! The next rally must commence in the same way but then you play to a front corner. He either fails to return it or hits up a weak shot. Furthermore, after this happens a few times he knows he has to return to a metre behind the "T" after every shot he hits and if you continue to hit from in front of him you know he will work harder than you will.

(d) *You are hitting shots down the side wall from the short line or a little further forward and he is hitting the ball before you can recover to the centre.*

Obviously he has positioned himself early towards the side wall to do this. If your court movements were based on the diagram on page 17 you would see him out of position as you move to hit the ball and a winning low cross-court shot or boast would be simple. However, even if you do not see him you must realise that your basic game has resulted in him taking a risk by getting out of position. Object achieved!

(e) *You are playing an opponent who is fast—possibly faster to the ball than you are—and is cutting off your shots down the wall and keeping you deep.*

It could be that he is better and more accurate in all departments than you are, but if you are hitting your shots deep, forcefully and accurately it is more likely you have made him take risks to cover your basic shot by guessing and thereby getting to the ball earlier. Object achieved! If he is cutting off your

The Australian women's team of 1971, with former British world champion Janet Shardlow (third from left). Demonstrating superb match play, the Australians made a clean sweep of the British test series. The players are (left to right): Marion Jackman, Heather McKay, Jenny Irving, Jean Walker and Mavis Nancarrow.

shots up near the short line your shot is hard and deep across-court. If he is coming in front of you but still back behind the service box you know his early movement and balance are towards the back of the court and a boast is your answer. Either of these alternatives present a possible winner, and at worst will put heavy pressure on him to reach your shot, so there's the possibility of a weak return. And certainly a few such shots will stop him from moving early, so your down-the-wall shots will again put pressure on him and you will take the centre of the court and resume smooth movement. [However you should first check that you are not at fault. See fault (a) on page 94.]

(f) *You are boasting or dropping to take your opponent forward early in the match and he is getting to the ball before you regain the centre.*

Your shot is good but you may be making it a little too far away from the centre, leaving yourself out of position. As it is early in the match it is probably accentuated because he is fresh and fast to the ball, stands well up on the "T", and likes being taken forward. Beware of this early pace. Make him stand

deep (with more deep shots) and only take him forward with long drops hugging the near wall or with accurate long boasts—at least until he has lost his early dash. If obvious drop shot opportunities are presented early in a match a good ploy is to approach the ball apparently poised for a drop shot, delay your shot until your opponent must move, then hit it deep to pass him and die before it hits a wall. The freshness of your opponent early in a match generally makes him feel confident of getting to the ball and hitting a winner from your drop shot and you should use this to your own advantage.

(g) *Your opponent is surprising you with his pace to the ball.*

It is likely he is moving early, so try to stop him from doing this by making quick judicious changes of direction with your shots. If you do this well and it fails to affect his speed to the ball you are playing against an extremely good player. Remember, you must always know where your opponent is, preferably by observation but failing this by the rapidity or otherwise with which he gets to his shots. This gives you the clue as to whether or not your

93

basic game is causing him to take risks and presenting you with the opportunity you are waiting for to vary play.

When you may be at fault

You must be able to read weaknesses in your own game, too. For example:

(a) *Your opponent dominates the centre of the court, has no trouble in cutting off your down-the-wall or cross-court shots and has you scrambling.*

Check your length; it is probably much too short. You must be feeding him with short shots to the danger area. Make him retreat at all costs by hitting harder and deeper down the wall.

(b) *Your opponent is volleying your cross-court shots.*

You are probably hitting too many shots across court, and probably from waist to shoulder high. Hit accurate length shots down the wall to make him cover them. Then when you are sure you can pass him, hit hard and low across court. From the front of the court you can also pull a fast cross-court shot to the nick at the service box to pass and go behind him.

(c) *You are on the defensive, scraping services off the back wall.*

You must attack your opponent's service. If possible volley before it hits the side wall. Failing that, volley after it hits the side wall. Only let it bounce if you know you can attack or hit a safe defensive shot taking your opponent away from the centre. You must do everything possible to upset the confidence and rhythm of an opponent who is making you play defensively off the back wall.

(d) *Your service is being attacked.*

This generally means your opponent is effectively volleying your service or you are hitting it so hard and high that it is bouncing too far across the court and too far forward off the back wall. For the first case serve a few fast ones straight at him from time to time to upset his attack, and make sure the remainder of your services hit the side wall. For the second case slow down your serve or hit the side wall lower down.

(e) *Your opponent is hitting unexpected winners from time to time or you are late to your shots.*

You are not watching him hit the ball or not getting back to the centre quickly enough.

ORIGINAL POSITION

(f) *You are making silly stroking mistakes: lifting your head and eyes off the ball too soon; lifting and turning your body towards the front wall as you make your shot; or rushing your stroking.*

The first two mistakes may originate from bad movement to the ball resulting in hitting from a cramped position. Move as shown in the diagram on page 17. Don't get too close to the ball. Practice playing with only a horizontal swing until your free stroking is functioning again. This procedure will also help to correct the third mistake, but primarily you must think of commencing your full swing before you reach your final hitting position and starting the horizontal swing as you reach it.

(g) *You are over-hitting.*

This is commonly caused by hitting hard when your weight is on your back foot and the ball is hit opposite it, or by moving in too close to the ball and hitting from a cramped position with your body facing the front wall. It can also be caused by hitting wildly. Face the side wall—comfortably away from the ball and with your weight on the front foot—and make your racket meet the ball in front of your front foot at a reduced pace until your length settles down.

(h) *You are inaccurate at hitting down the side wall.*

YES

NO

After playing a boast from the back forehand corner the player leaves her original position (far left). She moves at full speed (left) to take up a well-balanced volleying position inside the angle of the "T" on the forehand side, and her opponent will find it extremely difficult to place the ball out of her reach on either side. The player (above) takes a straight path from her original position towards a possible short shot on the backhand wall, leaving the whole of the forehand court unguarded against an attacking shot.

This is generally caused by facing the front wall. Turn and face the side wall and keep your body out of the shot. It may also be caused by not leading with your elbow as your stroke approaches the ball.

(i) *You are making mistakes on volleys and drop shots when the ball comes to you quickly.*

You are probably trying to make the ideal placement when due to the pace of the ball the stroke is just not "on". When a shot comes to you quickly you must settle for the best shot that *is* "on", not the dream shot that has one chance in 10 of succeeding. Your instinctive safe shot is a firmly hit ball that is sufficiently up the front wall to take it to whichever

back corner it can be safely directed. However, if your opponent is still deep and out of position, and you have time, hit a volley or drop shot short to the nick on whatever side is "on". You must also check that you are holding your racket vertically while waiting for a volley. Trailing your racket early makes you late to the ball.

(j) *You play attacking boasts from the back of the court and find your opponent's drop shot or passing shot beats you.*

When you play this boast you must move very quickly and be well balanced right up in the angle of the "T" opposite to your opponent when he makes his shot. From this position you can volley virtually any cross-court shot (which you are looking for) or get quickly up the centre to a drop shot. Despite the fact that you are not on the centre line, your position enables you to cover a shot down the wall and if you are still moving when your opponent hits his shot you have given yourself the best chance of covering any return.

(k) *Both you and your opponent are scrambling to get to shots in a rally up the front of the court.*

Your predominant aim must be to get to the ball early enough to hit it down the court past him. Don't over-hit; just get it past him so that he cannot reach it. A drop shot should follow a drop shot only when your opponent has become sufficiently committed to returning to the centre to make it impossible for him to reach another drop shot. If you are both forward your priorities are: (i) a length passing shot, (ii) a lob, (iii) a drop shot in the corner farthest from your opponent, (iv) a drop shot to wherever you can hit it.

(l) *A big, strong opponent is planting his feet firmly, hitting the ball like a bullet, and recovering slowly.*

You are not making him run to the ball. Get to it as quickly as possible and hit it away from him. Make him run fast to the ball and the odds are you will destroy his game.

(m) *Your previous shot has not taken your opponent sufficiently away from the centre to enable you to have easy access to certain parts of the court.*

Whatever you do, you must not stand too close to him when he plays his shot. For quick access and a clear view of the ball, stand away from him. From this position you can move early and at full pace in whatever direction you see is necessary, instead of starting late, after a bad view of the ball, and changing direction to avoid interference.

WHEN THE GOING IS TOUGH

There are times when your immediate strategy can win or lose a match. For example, you and your opponent are experienced match-players and, after a long struggle, you are 5-all in the fifth game of a hard-fought match. You feel ready to die and still your opponent won't give in. What are you thinking? What should you do?

1. Do not give the slightest indication in your actions of your own condition or worries. Think clearly about your strokes and tactics, and do not make emotional outbursts.

2. Convince yourself that no matter how bad you feel, your opponent must feel worse. Remember, if he feels as bad as you do, the next rally may be his last throw. Wait for him to misjudge or mistime—this is the sign you are looking for.

3. Concentrate on watching the ball and your balance. As your pace has gone, concentrate more than ever on your stroke play, making him run maximum distance in minimum time. This is your most potent weapon.

4. Don't try desperate shots. Play tight and wait for a loose one. You may be unlucky, but usually you won't.

5. Try to make your shots, including short ones, finish low on a wall, particularly the forehand wall. This produces errors from a tired opponent.

6. At this stage of the match the first good short shot from deep in the court when you are both there often wins the rally. But, be sure you are balanced when you try it.

7. If you are out of position always play a shot that gives you ample time to regain position.

8. Don't serve over the top or serve an easy volley.

TIPS FOR MATCH PLAY

You will save yourself a lot of time in polishing your game if you take advantage of the following tips:

1. Study your opponent's game. Most players have some stance, backswing, foot placement or mannerism which indicates that a certain shot will be played—watch for it.

2. Anticipation comes only from watching your opponent hit the ball. Always do this and it will gradually develop.

3. Don't overrun the ball when you are moving to it. Pause before you hit so you retain your balance and accuracy.

4. A smash is not generally a winner. Place it and be ready for it to come back. Play the shot with a short backswing and hit the ball well ahead if you want to restrict the bounce.

5. If you are tired and want to save your legs for a while, keep the ball close and deep on the side wall or alternatively, provided you are in a position to do so, keep on lobbing it high into the corners.

6. Don't look for easy winners because in top squash they are just not there. Anticipate that you will have long rallies and patiently wait for the right shot to hit for a winner.

YES

NO

The non-striker (above) stands well clear of the striker so that he has a good view of the ball, is well balanced for quick movement, and can move to an attacking position on either side of his opponent if the ball is hit down a side wall. The non-striker (left) is too close to his opponent, doesn't have a clear view of the ball, and is badly balanced because he has to lean back to keep clear of his opponent's racket. If the ball is hit down the wall he will have to move sideways to clear his opponent and will lose any opportunity to attack.

7. Watch for weaknesses in your opponent such as a dislike of a certain type of service, bad positioning, faulty production of a certain stroke, or lack of court speed which can be exploited by playing short shots. Many players can not move up and down a court as easily as they can move across it. If an opponent recovers slowly after hitting a ball, bustle him. Watch for any dislike of either hard or softly hit shots or lack of stamina. (In the latter case you should, of course, never let the opponent stay still.)

8. If you find your opponent's accuracy too much for you, try to break it up by changing your game completely. Alter your pace and strategy in the hope it will unsettle him. It may even pay to lob every shot you can to upset his rhythm. Once you shake his confidence you are "back in the game".

9. The player who has plenty of time to make his shots is the one who will apply accurate pressure and win. Give yourself plenty of time by using a searching basic game, good court position and quick movement to your shots.

10. If you ease up and lose control of a squash match you'll find it exceedingly difficult to regain—so never lose control.

11. Don't practise with a slower ball than you are likely to play with in a match. If you have an important match coming up practise several times on the court on which it will be played to familiarise yourself with the lighting and the pace of the floor and walls.

12. In hitting up before a match commences endeavour to get your length and your correct timing and placement of the ball. Try to hit the ball right back to the corners, both from centre court and from back near the corners because you will be forced to hit shots from there. Try boasts in order to get the length of a boast from the back of the court and the "feel" of the walls. If you get the length of your drive and length of your boast from deep in the court you will have covered the two shots that require the most "settling in to". You should also use your hit up to find out a bit about your opponent. Lob him a few, hit him a few hard ones in a few different places, and observe his reaction—you can often learn a lot from it. Make sure you assess the pace of the ball, the floor and the walls. If you consider the ball unsuitable, discuss the matter with your opponent. You may jointly or individually protest to the referee.

13. Try to win the first half-dozen rallies, but don't become "over careful" if you play badly early. Beat your opponent to the punch if possible. If you feel your opponent will beat you, go all out to win the first game and hence confidence.

14. If you have kept your opponent at the wrong end of a hard rally and won it, follow up immediately with bustling and volleying before he regains his composure.

15. Being down 2-nil and 8-love presents great possibilities. Think how worried your opponent will be if you win the third game!

16. Wear lightweight shoes. Never wear brand new shoes in a match. If your feet get tender wear two pairs of socks with foot powder sprinkled inside.

17. Liking for racket type varies. Generally a racket with about centre-balance and weighing around 200g (7-7¼oz) is recommended. If you want more pace in your game you should have your racket strung more tightly. Loose stringing is good for control of drop shots, but if too loose cuts down your pace-through-timing. Don't build up your racket grip—the small grip is better suited to squash stroking.

Ken Hiscoe, perfectly poised to do either a drop shot or a length shot to the front wall. A former Australian and world amateur champion, Ken's ability to vary front wall shots gave him consistent winners from this position.

TRAINING AND NUTRITION

Squash requires a high level of both technical skill and physical fitness.

Although priority must always be given to mastering the skills of the game, physical fitness is nonetheless so essential that you must have a potentially high physical capacity—speed, stamina, etc—to have any prospect of reaching championship level. But beware! The reward for concentrating from the start on physical fitness rather than cultivating technical skill may be only that it takes 10 minutes longer to be beaten. Without complete skill there is no future.

The basics of a sound training and nutrition program for squash are:

1. Playing and simulating squash is the best training.
2. Off-the-court stamina training and power build-up should be done mainly in the off to pre-season months.
3. Dedication, self-motivation, a suitable lifestyle, adequate practice facilities, tigerish footwork, speed and good general athletic ability are essential.
4. Both anaerobic and aerobic energy systems must be developed.
5. Interval training adapted to squash should be followed in off-the-court training.
6. Guidelines should be used to check that intensity of work in training is correct.
7. You should take it easy during the first few weeks of training to avoid muscle strain or damage.
8. Interval skipping associated with 5-BX (males) or X-BX (females) or other properly prescribed exercises must be done daily throughout the season.
9. Never play lazy squash. Follow the on-the-court training on page 113.
10. When training or playing makes you feel jaded and reduces your efficiency the more you try, you should take a break.
11. A well-balanced diet is essential, with special considerations being adhered to for serious competition.
12. An increase in protein diet during pre-season stamina build-up is advisable for younger, growing athletes and helpful for others.
13. A carbohydrate diet is recommended for match-play with a special one-week diet preparation as a build-up for an important event.
14. You should not dry out before a match.
15. Fluid intake is advisable during a long match.

TRAINING

Before undertaking a serious training program there are several important questions you must ask yourself:

1. Are you prepared to dedicate yourself to achieving championship status or do you lack any real motivation and the ability to finally stand on your own feet in tough competition?
2. What is your lifestyle? Will you survive the rigours of adhering to a reasonably strict diet, not smoking, drinking little alcohol, and getting plenty of study and practice?
3. Does the necessity to give your best on a big occasion make or break you?
4. Are your facilities for practice and training adequate?
5. Is your game technically sound or in the process of becoming so?
6. Are you a good or potentially good athlete and could any physical weaknesses be remedied by suitable exercises?

If you have answered all these questions satisfactorily, you must now consider exactly what training program you are going to undertake. This is an individual matter but the basic theories and guidelines set out here will enable you to plan a program to suit your particular needs and make the most of your game.

The basic theory

Professor F. Cotton, whose theories in the 1950s revitalised most sports training in this country and brought Australian swimmers to a standard of physical fitness unequalled anywhere in the world at that time, believed that the best way to train for any game was to play that game.

After analysing a game of squash he said that if you haven't time to spend playing squash you should exercise in a manner which simulates the actions you'd go through on a squash court. In the same way as boxers shadow spar you should get a racket and get out in the open and go right through an imaginary match. Do everything you should do on a squash court. Imagine you are playing an opponent and he is putting you through the troubles you would meet during a match.

Professor Cotton did not believe running or road work were good training for squash for the simple reason that the whole manner of movement, breathing and exercise is different. He pointed out that in squash you move quickly for a while then stop. Then you move again and stop, and so on. You do not continually run forward as in running; you go backwards, forwards and all over the court.

He considered skipping to be a far better form of training for squash. Boxers, whose footwork is very similar to that of squash players, he said, use skipping as an important part of their training. They skip backwards and forwards and "feel" the floor every time they move, and finally develop an ability to automatically time their contact with it. Professor Cotton believed this to be the ideal training for squash and recommended that the skipping not be continuous, but in bursts of the average duration of a squash rally and with short breaks between each burst.

Many training methods based on this general theory have been researched and applied to several sports during recent years resulting in continually improved performances. Unfortunately, the many peculiarities of squash, e.g. the mix of full pressure and rest, invalidate the use of training programs prepared for other sports. The program presented here is a basic guideline developed from studying modern methods of training, present-day requirements of championship squash and my own experience in both championship athletics and championship squash.

Competitions in Australia often run from 1 March to 30 November, leaving three summer months clear. After tapering off with the odd social game, championship contenders should have a complete break away from the court for 4-6 weeks ending the last week in January. Those who are enthusiastically building up their skills and not yet ready to compete in championships should take a minimum break and use the three months to build up their game, making any major technical changes that may be necessary but which are difficult to make during the competitive season.

Energy

I extend my warmest thanks to Dr Frank Pyke of the University of Western Australia from whose paper "Strategy of Training", presented at the national seminar for sports coaches organised by the Australian Department of Tourism and Recreation and the Australian Sports Council in Melbourne during May 1975, I have extracted in substance the material on energy and accepted valuable guidance on other aspects of training. (For the full paper see Sports Coaching, Australian Government Publishing Service, Canberra 1976.)

Energy is a basic factor in sports performance and it is therefore advisable to understand its fundamentals before undertaking a rigorous training program.

Energy for activity is provided by the breakdown of adenosine triphosphate (ATP) which is stored in short supply in the muscles. Because it is capable of allowing movement to continue for only a second or two, ATP must be replaced by other processes.

The largest quantity of ATP is provided when oxygen (aerobic energy) is present. However, because the muscles do not store much oxygen and because it takes a little over a minute for the circulation to transport enough oxygen to even start to satisfy their demands, there are two other emergency energy systems, called anaerobic (without oxygen) systems, available.

Let us look at the two systems a little more closely (as energy systems overlap, the times given are those when they predominate):

1. **Anaerobic energy**

    (a) *Phosphate energy:* This is the explosive energy used in a 100-metre dash. A breakdown of high energy phosphate compounds stored in the muscles, it supports full activity for 5-10 seconds and helps maintain activity for up to 30 seconds. Phosphate energy has the great advantage that it can be rapidly replenished on resting (a little after 10 seconds, 50 per cent after 30 seconds, 75 per cent after one minute and 100 per cent after two minutes). This makes it possible to repeat short bursts without becoming exhausted.

    (b) *Lactic acid energy:* After 10 seconds of full effort or up to 30 seconds of minor or intermittent effort, lactic acid energy becomes the predominate energy supply for about the next 90 seconds. This energy is manufactured from glucose (sugar), which is broken down to lactic acid. Unlike phosphate energy, however, lactic energy has the disadvantage that the lactic acid does not disperse quickly on rest but remains in the muscles and produces fatigue. Large amounts of lactic acid can take more than an hour to disperse, so recovery is much slower.

2. **Aerobic energy**

    When the duration of intensive work is prolonged, more dependence is placed on the lungs, heart, blood and blood vessels to transport oxygen from the air to the muscles, and on the muscles to utilise the oxygen presented to them. Both sugar and fat fuel can now be oxidised and a significant quantity of energy released without requiring anaerobic assistance. Opinion is divided as to the time before aerobic (oxygen) energy predominates in continuous work, some researchers saying two minutes, others three.

Accurate charts have been prepared for the relative uses of phosphate, lactic acid and oxygen energy for running, swimming and many "continuous" sports, and much research has been carried out on field sports, such as football, with regard to position on the field. However, in this regard there has been little in-depth study into squash.

The 3-5 seconds average interval between rallies does not appear to provide any energy recuperative time but merely a diminishing of work intensity. However, because of the recuperative powers of phosphate energy it seems the second, third and fourth games in squash could commence with a 75 per cent normal supply of phosphate energy and the fifth game with a 100 per cent supply due to the intervals between games. Lactic acid energy would show no signs of recuperation and become more and more an element of fatigue.

The training program given here is based on placing main emphasis on oxygen energy in the off-season, and gradually changing to 30 per cent phosphate energy, 30 per cent lactic energy and 40 per cent oxygen energy by the commencement of the playing season.

Interval Training

As its name implies, interval training involves alternating periods of work (exercise) and recovery (relief or rest). It has many advantages over continuous training, the main one being that more work can be done with less fatigue. For example, a person who runs as fast as possible for one minute will finish exhausted due to the build up of lactic acid. The same person could, by running 10 seconds at a time and having 30 seconds rest in between, finish one minute's exercise comparatively fresh because only a small amount of lactic acid would be produced. Each rest period has enabled sufficient phosphate energy to be built up again to produce most of the energy used in the work.

This principle applies equally to longer, slower training. As the length of the work period increases and the intensity of the work decreases, the relative relief period can be reduced. The ratio of work to relief would be initially 1:2, then 1:1, and perhaps even 1:½.

Training on these lines enables an athlete, for example, to cover a certain distance at a total of near-record time but with rest periods which considerably reduce fatigue and make work intensity higher. As he improves, the relief periods can be gradually shortened until they no longer exist. Alternatively, he could maintain relief periods and build up more distance or cover each distance more rapidly.

The most important feature of the interval training system is that the saving in fatigue can be converted to an intensification of the work program. Research indicates that as much as two-and-a-half times the intensity level of "continuous" training can be reached before comparable levels of fatigue are reached. Further, it is claimed that the intensity of the work performed during interval training sessions is directly related to the amount by which the energy capacities of the muscles improve.

Another advantage of interval training is that the stroke volume (the amount of blood pumped by the heart each heart beat or stroke) is highest not during exercise but during the recovery period from exercise. So, as the higher the stroke volume the higher the capacity of the aerobic system (because more oxygen is transported to the working muscles), interval training which has intermittent exercise with regular recovery periods takes the heart pumping volume to a maximum more often than does "continuous" training.

Thus, interval training does a great deal to improve the capacity of the oxygen system. The continuous hard-slog types of training, though having certain other advantages, should be used only in off-season periods and then preferably not overdone.

In summary, the advantages of the interval training system in regard to the development of the energy systems are:

1. It allows phosphate energy to be used repeatedly. This provides an adequate stimulus for promoting an increase in the energy capacity of this system and aids in delaying the onset of fatigue by not delving so deeply into the lactic acid system.
2. With proper regulation of the duration and type of relief interval, the involvement of the lactic acid system will be greater, and thus improved.
3. By working long enough at a sufficient intensity and by improving the maximal attainable stroke volume through the rest periods following work, the aerobic system is developed.

Types of training for squash

The recommended training for top-grade squash can be divided into four categories:

1. On-the-court practising with a ball to improve skills and match play. This has been dealt with at length in the text of previous chapters.
2. Practising without a ball, either on the court or elsewhere, but simulating all or some portion of a game to improve technique. This is set out as exercises at the end of the chapter on court movement (see page 23) and supplemented by exercises in the interval training programs detailed later in this chapter.
3. Running using interval training (five days a week during the pre-season, tapering off after 13 weeks to lighter work during the main season) to develop and maintain the capacity of energy sources and improve speed and movement.
4. General flexibility or light development exercises and any exercises necessary to remedy obvious physical deficiences and build up power or pace.

With a short off-season much reliance is placed on continuous play and light remedial exercises to remedy most physical weaknesses applicable to squash. However there are cases where squash can be suspended or taken very lightly with benefit while other concentrated training is undertaken to remedy a weakness. Such training should be discontinued or tapered off as soon as the direct squash training outlined in this book is commenced. Weaknesses are generally related to pace, power or stamina and could apply to, for example, players who have attained their rank by sheer racket ability but lack athletic ability in other physical senses.

For pace, try a period of athletic sprint training and competition in spiked shoes for general sharpening, including pace off the mark.

For general muscular power, light weight-lifting has been used by at least one champion but expert advice is required. There are many forms of exercise to choose from, but remember that every exercise you do must have some ultimate relevance to squash.

For general conditioning and flexibility, the Canadian Air Force 5-BX (males) and X-BX (females) exercises are excellent, particularly if you apply the principles of interval training to them.

For stamina you need heavy training, preferably playing a lot of squash but a period of long distance running is also useful. If you have never been subjected to stamina-oriented exercise in your youth and show both mental and physical weakness in tough physical encounters, a few months of long distance running could be of great value. If the case is serious enough and you are otherwise a potential champion a six-month season of training and competing at long distance track or cross-country running will have valuable physical benefits and, because of competition, improve your mental determination to fight fatigue and stay with an opponent. Never lose sight of the fact that this training is remedial training only and is not part of a basic annual training schedule for squash. In the program set out later in this chapter provision has been made for the work load to be adjusted according to the capacity of the player. If maximum capacity is attained there is not much more that can be done, nor can energy be better applied to prepare you for competitive squash.

Your training program

A single training program can not suit the needs of every individual. For this reason the specimen off-the-court training programs in this chapter have been designed so you can adapt them to your own particular needs.

Two base sets of times-for-distances are specified, class A and class B, the latter being an average level for most players. Give yourself an adequate trial to assess your condition then relate your program to the classification closest to your ability.

If you are a top-class athlete you may find the program inadequate and may have to either increase distances or number of repetitions or have relatively faster times, or both. On the other hand, after a fair trial, you may have to do the opposite. However, always show a preference for pace rather than distance during the competitive squash season.

The "track" ability of players will vary considerably in terms of times. The majority of people find class B times a suitable basis. The time at players' disposal and their opportunity to relax will vary. Physical ability and opportunity to rest may make it possible to carry a program of three track days a week further into the squash season than is shown in the program, but any such course should be approached cautiously and great care taken to see that track training is not reducing the far more important court training. Always beware of taking any heavy track training in the period approaching important squash events.

Throughout your training you must continually check the adequacy of your work load and adjust the program to suit your capabilities. If your work load is inappropriate you must increase or decrease it in relation to the class A or class B times on which you are basing your program.

Work intensity guidelines

The following guidelines enable you to regularly check if your program is providing you with an adequate, excessive or insufficient work rate so you can make any adjustments:

1. Reasonable heart rates during the interval training program work periods measured at the commencement of intervals are (for both men and women):

Age	Heart rate (beats per minute)
Under 20 years	190
20-29 years	180
30-39 years	170
40-49 years	160
50-59 years	150
60-69 years	140

2. If identical work rates (i.e. intensity, duration, etc) are followed and the heart rate—taken 1-1½ minutes after the cessation of the last run of the work-out on several occasions—is decreasing, an increase in the work load is necessary.

3. Reasonable heart rates to which heart beats should drop at the end of a relief period and prior to starting the next repetition or bracket during the interval training programs (for both men and women) are:

Age	Heart rate (beats per minute)	
	between repetitions	between brackets
Under 20 years	150	125
20-29 years	140	120
30-39 years	130	110
40-49 years	120	105
50-59 years	115	100
60-69 years	105	90

Although relief intervals are not shown between brackets in the interval training programs, you should work out suitable rest periods for yourself according to the drop in heart beats recommended in guideline 3 above.

Off-the-court interval training programs

Commence your training program two months before early season matches.

Times and, in special cases, distances, are subject to modification to your own needs (see the above guidelines). Except for 20-metre sprints, all times are from easy moving starts.

There are separate interval training programs (ITPs) for men and women, and times are given for class A and class B according to ability. After a reasonable trial, relate your program to either A or B and apply the guidelines to prepare your final program.

Where R is shown the relief should be rest-relief, i.e. walk or flex between work.

Where W is shown the relief should be work-relief, i.e. light to mild exercise (including jogging).

Relief periods are not shown between "brackets" but intervals between repetitions would normally be used unless a longer period is needed to allow the heart beat to drop as in guideline 3 on page 105.

If you find by experience that the longer intervals provide too much rest you may cut them to as little as three minutes.

The Canadian Air Force 5-BX or X-BX exercises plus skipping should be done daily in addition to your Interval Training Program.

MALE SQUASH INTERVAL TRAINING PROGRAM

Day	Daily Schedule		Distance in Metres	Time	Work Relief Ratio
	First Week				
1	Bracket 1.	2 runs	400	easy	1:3 W
	" 2.	8 runs	100	easy	1:3 R
2	Bracket 1.	2 runs	400	easy	1:3 W
	" 2.	4 runs	200	easy	1:3 R
3	Bracket 1.	3 runs	400	easy	1:3 W
	" 2.	4 runs	200	easy	1:3 R
4	Bracket 1.	1 run	800	easy	1:2 R
	" 2.	6 runs	200	easy	1:3 W
	Second Week				
1	Bracket 1.	2 runs	800	easy	1:2 R
	" 2.	2 runs	400	easy	1:3 W
2	Bracket 1.	2 runs	800	easy	1:2 R
	" 2.	3 runs	400	easy	1:3 W
3	Bracket 1.	2 runs	800	easy	1:2 R
	" 2.	5 runs	400	easy	1:3 W
4	Bracket 1.	3 runs	800	easy	1:2 R
	" 2.	3 runs	400	easy	1:3 W
5	Bracket 1.	1 run	3,200	easy	1:1 R

Day	Daily Schedule		Distance in Metres	Time* A	Time* B	Relief between Repetitions*
	Third Week					
1	Bracket 1.	2 runs	800	2.45	3.00	3.30 R
	" 2.	2 runs	400	1.15	1.20	2.40 W
2	Bracket 1.	1 run	2,400	10.00	11.00	6.30 R
	" 2.	2 runs	100	0.16	0.17	1.00 R
3	Bracket 1.	2 runs	600	1.56	2.12	3.00 W
	" 2.	4 runs	200	0.33	0.37	1.50 W
	" 3.	4 runs	200	0.33	0.37	1.50 W
4	Bracket 1.	1 run	800	2.40	2.55	3.30 R
	" 2.	2 runs	400	1.12	1.19	2.30 W
	" 3.	4 runs	200	0.33	0.36	1.50 W
5	Bracket 1.	1 run	3,200	13.20	15.00	7.30 R
	" 2.	4 runs	100	0.16	0.17	1.00 R
	Fourth Week					
1	Bracket 1.	2 runs	1,600	6.10	6.30	5.00 R
	" 2.	2 runs	100	0.16	0.17	1.00 R
2	Bracket 1.	3 runs	800	2.35	2.50	3.00 R
	" 2.	4 runs	200	0.32	0.35	1.45 W
3	Bracket 1.	4 runs	200	0.32	0.35	1.45 W
	" 2.	4 runs	200	0.32	0.35	1.45 W
	" 3.	4 runs	200	0.32	0.35	1.45 W
	" 4.	4 runs	200	0.32	0.35	1.45 W
4	Bracket 1.	1 run	3,200	13.00	14.30	7.00 R
	" 2.	4 runs	100	0.16	0.17	0.50 R
5	Bracket 1.	1 run	3,200	13.00	14.30	7.00 R
	" 2.	4 runs	100	0.16	0.17	0.50 R

* Minutes and seconds

Day	Daily Schedule		Distance in Metres	Time* A	B	Relief between Repetitions*
	Fifth Week					
1	Bracket 1.	4 runs	800	2.30	2.50	3.00 R
	" 2.	4 runs	100	0.15	0.16	0.50 R
2	Bracket 1.	2 runs	1,600	6.00	6.15	5.00 R
	" 2.	4 runs	100	0.15	0.16	0.50 R
3	Bracket 1.	3 runs	600	1.45	2.00	2.45 W
	" 2.	4 runs	200	0.31	0.34	1.45 W
	" 3.	4 runs	200	0.31	0.34	1.45 W
4	Bracket 1.	1 run	3,200	13.00	14.00	7.00 R
	" 2.	4 runs	100	0.15	0.16	0.50 R
5	Bracket 1.	1 run	2,400	9.30	10.00	6.00 R
	" 2.	4 runs	200	0.30	0.33	1.40 W
	" 3.	4 runs	100	0.15	0.16	0.50 R
	Sixth Week					
1	Bracket 1.	3 runs	800	2.25	2.45	3.00 R
	" 2.	8 runs	50	0.07	0.08	0.30 R
	" 3.	4 runs	90 slalom	easy	easy	1.00 R

Note: The 90-metre slalom is run carrying a racket at approx. 90 degrees to forearm over a 30-metre course with two complete about-turns. Eight stakes are placed in a straight line at 3-metre intervals, with 4½ metres clear at each end of the stakes. Pass successive stakes on different sides (you must sidestep or swerve around them). At the 30-metre mark prop with both feet level and, starting with knees well bent, turn using your hips and pass each stake on the opposite side on the way back. Each of the 30-metre turns must be made in a different direction (clockwise or anti-clockwise).

Day	Daily Schedule		Distance in Metres	Time* A	B	Relief between Repetitions*
2	Bracket 1.	1 run	3,200	12.45	13.45	7.00 R
	" 2.	8 runs	50	0.06	0.07	0.30 R
	" 3.	8 runs	90 slalom	easy	easy	1.00 R
3	Bracket 1.	8 runs	200	0.29	0.32	1.40 W
	" 2.	8 runs	100	0.15	0.16	0.50 R
	" 3.	5 runs	20	full speed from starting blocks (walk back and repeat)		R
	" 4.	8 runs	90 slalom	½ speed		1.00 R
4	Bracket 1.	1 run	2,400	9.15	9.45	5.30 R
	" 2.	5 runs	20	full speed S/Bs (walk back and repeat)		R
	" 3.	8 runs	90 slalom	½ speed		1.00 R
5	Bracket 1.	1 run	800	2.25	2.45	3.00 R
	" 2.	10 runs	90 slalom	¾ speed		1.00 R
	" 3.		15 minutes continuous playing with partner without ball on approx. court size			3.00 R
	" 4.		10 minutes each Phantom Squash on approx. court size, each rally of approx. 10 strokes – continuous			3.00 R

Note: If you do not have a partner for Phantom Squash and 15 minutes of playing without the ball, substitute 20 minutes of continuous, meticulous shadow-sparring with 4-second intervals between rallies.

Day	Daily Schedule		Distance in Metres	Time* A	B	Relief between Repetitions*
	Seventh Week					
1	Bracket 1.	3 runs	800	2.25	2.45	3.00 R
	" 2.	6 runs	100	0.15	0.16	0.50 R
	" 3.	6 runs	20	full speed S/Bs (walk back and repeat)		R
	" 4.	6 runs	20	full speed S/Bs (walk back and repeat)		R
	" 5.	10 runs	90 slalom	¾ speed		1.00 R
2	Bracket 1.	4 runs	600	1.40	1.55	2.45 W
	" 2.	6 runs	100	0.15	0.16	0.50 R
	" 3.	6 runs	20	full speed S/Bs (walk back and repeat)		R
	" 4.	6 runs	20	full speed S/Bs (walk back and repeat)		R
	" 5.	6 runs	90 slalom	full and ¾ speed		1.00 R
	" 6.	6 runs	90 slalom	full and ¾ speed		1.00 R

Note: Where slalom is at full and ¾ speed, make the two complete about-turns and the centre lap at full speed and the remainder at ¾ speed.

* Minutes and seconds

Day	Daily Schedule		Distance in Metres	Time* A	Time* B	Relief between Repetitions*
3	Bracket 1.	4 runs	200	0.28	0.32	1.40 W
	" 2.	4 runs	200	0.28	0.32	1.40 W
	" 3.	6 runs	20	full speed S/Bs		
				(walk back and repeat)		R
	" 4.	6 runs	20	full speed S/Bs		
				(walk back and repeat)		R
	" 5.	6 runs	90 slalom	full and ¾ speed		1.00 R
	" 6.	6 runs	90 slalom	full and ¾ speed		1.00 R
	" 7.	10 minutes each Phantom Squash, each rally approx. 10 strokes – continuous				3.00 R
4	Bracket 1.	1 run	1,600	5.45	6.00	5.00 R
	" 2.	4 runs	100	0.14	0.15	0.45 R
	" 3.	6 runs	20	full speed S/Bs		
				(walk back and repeat)		R
	" 4.	6 runs	20	full speed S/Bs		
				(walk back and repeat)		R
	" 5.	6 runs	90 slalom	full and ¾ speed		1.00 R
	" 6.	6 runs	90 slalom	full and ¾ speed		1.00 R
	" 7.	10 minutes each Phantom Squash, each rally of approx. 10 strokes – continuous				3.00 R
5	Bracket 1.	1 run	800	2.20	2.40	3.00 R
	" 2.	6 runs	90 slalom	full and ¾ speed		1.00 R
	" 3.	6 runs	90 slalom	full and ¾ speed		1.00 R
	" 4.	15 minutes continuous playing without ball				3.00 R
	" 5.	10 minutes each Phantom Squash, each rally approx. 10 strokes – continuous				3.00 R

Eighth Week

Day	Daily Schedule		Distance in Metres	Time* A	Time* B	Relief between Repetitions*
1	Bracket 1.	3 runs	800	2.18	2.37	3.00 R
	" 2.	6 runs	100	0.14	0.15	0.45 R
	" 3.	6 runs	20	full speed S/Bs		
				(walk back and repeat)		R
	" 4.	6 runs	20	full speed S/Bs		
				(walk back and repeat)		R
	" 5.	6 runs	90 slalom	full and ¾ speed		1.00 R
	" 6.	6 runs	90 slalom	full and ¾ speed		1.00 R
2	Bracket 1.	4 runs	600	1.35	1.50	2.45 W
	" 2.	6 runs	100	0.14	0.15	0.45 R
	" 3.	6 runs	20	full speed S/Bs		
				(walk back and repeat)		R
	" 4.	6 runs	20	full speed S/Bs		
				(walk back and repeat)		R
	" 5.	6 runs	90 slalom	full and ¾ speed		1.00 R
	" 6.	6 runs	90 slalom	full and ¾ speed		1.00 R
3	Bracket 1.	4 runs	200	0.28	0.32	1.40 W
	" 2.	4 runs	200	0.28	0.32	1.40 W
	" 3.	6 runs	20	full speed S/Bs		
				(walk back and repeat)		R
	" 4.	6 runs	20	full speed S/Bs		
				(walk back and repeat)		R
	" 5.	6 runs	90 slalom	full and ¾ speed		1.00 R
	" 6.	6 runs	90 slalom	full and ¾ speed		1.00 R
	" 7.	10 minutes each Phantom Squash, each rally approx. 10 strokes – continuous				3.00 R
4	Bracket 1.	1 run	1,600	5.30	5.45	5.00 R
	" 2.	4 runs	100	0.14	0.15	0.45 R
	" 3.	6 runs	20	full speed S/Bs		
				(walk back and repeat)		R
	" 4.	6 runs	20	full speed S/Bs		
				(walk back and repeat)		R
	" 5.	6 runs	90 slalom	full and ¾ speed		1.00 R
	" 6.	6 runs	90 slalom	full and ¾ speed		1.00 R
	" 7.	10 minutes each Phantom Squash, each rally approx. 10 strokes – continuous				3.00 R
5	Bracket 1.	1 run	800	2.15	2.35	3.00 R
	" 2.	6 runs	90 slalom	full and ¾ speed		1.00 R
	" 3.	6 runs	90 slalom	full and ¾ speed		1.00 R
	" 4.	15 minutes continuous playing without ball				3.00 R
	" 5.	10 minutes each Phantom Squash, each rally approx. 10 strokes – continuous				

* Minutes and seconds

FEMALE SQUASH INTERVAL TRAINING PROGRAM

Day	Daily Schedule	Distance in Metres	Time	Work Relief Ratio
	First Week			
1	Bracket 1. 2 runs	400	easy	1:3 W
	" 2. 8 runs	100	easy	1:3 R
2	Bracket 1. 2 runs	400	easy	1:3 W
	" 2. 4 runs	200	easy	1:3 R
3	Bracket 1. 3 runs	400	easy	1:3 W
	" 2. 4 runs	200	easy	1:3 W
4	Bracket 1. 1 run	800	easy	1:3 R
	" 2. 6 runs	200	easy	1:3 W
	Second Week			
1	Bracket 1. 2 runs	800	easy	1:3 R
	" 2. 1 run	400	easy	1:3 W
2	Bracket 1. 5 runs	400	easy	1:3 W
3	Bracket 1. 2 runs	800	easy	1:3 R
	" 2. 2 runs	400	easy	1:3 W
4	Bracket 1. 3 runs	800	easy	1:3 R
	" 2. 1 run	400	easy	1:3 W
5	Bracket 1. 1 run	2,400	easy	1:2 R

Day	Daily Schedule	Distance in Metres	Time* A	Time* B	Relief between Repetitions*
	Third Week				
1	Bracket 1. 2 runs	800	3.20	3.40	3.45 R
	" 2. 4 runs	100	0.18	0.19	1.00 R
2	Bracket 1. 1 run	2,400	11.20	12.15	8.00 R
	" 2. 2 runs	100	0.18	0.19	1.00 R
3	Bracket 1. 2 runs	600	2.18	2.32	3.30 W
	" 2. 8 runs	100	0.18	0.19	1.00 R
4	Bracket 1. 1 run	3,200	16.00	18.00	10.00 R
	" 2. 4 runs	100	0.18	0.19	1.00 R
5	Bracket 1. 2 runs	800	3.15	3.35	3.45 R
	" 2. 6 runs	200	0.37	0.39	2.00 W
	Fourth Week				
1	Bracket 1. 1 run	2,400	11.05	12.00	8.00 R
	" 2. 4 runs	100	0.18	0.19	1.00 R
2	Bracket 1. 3 runs	800	3.10	3.30	3.30 R
	" 2. 4 runs	200	0.36	0.38	2.00 W
3	Bracket 1. 1 run	3,200	15.30	17.30	10.00 R
	" 2. 4 runs	100	0.18	0.19	1.00 R
4	Bracket 1. 2 runs	800	3.10	3.30	3.30 R
	" 2. 6 runs	200	0.36	0.38	2.00 W
5	Bracket 1. 1 run	2,400	10.50	11.45	8.00 R
	" 2. 4 runs	100	0.18	0.19	1.00 R
	Fifth Week				
1	Bracket 1. 3 runs	800	3.05	3.25	3.30 R
	" 2. 8 runs	50	0.08	0.09	0.30 R
	" 3. 2 runs	100	0.17	0.18	0.55 R
2	Bracket 1. 1 run	1,600	6.45	7.15	6.00 R
	" 2. 8 runs	50	0.08	0.09	0.30 R
	" 3. 1 run	400	1.22	1.30	2.50 W
	" 4. 4 runs	100	0.17	0.18	0.55 R
3	Bracket 1. 1 run	3,200	15.00	17.00	10.00 R
	" 2. 8 runs	50	0.08	0.09	0.30 R
4	Bracket 1. 3 runs	800	3.05	3.25	3.30 R
	" 2. 8 runs	50	0.07	0.08	0.30 R
	" 3. 4 runs	100	0.17	0.18	0.55 R

* Minutes and seconds

Day	Daily Schedule		Distance in Metres	Time* A	B	Relief between Repetitions*
5	Bracket 1.	2 runs	600	2.10	2.25	3.00 W
	" 2.	4 runs	200	0.36	0.38	2.00 W
	" 3.	4 runs	90 slalom	easy	easy	1.00 R

Note: The 90-metre slalom is run carrying a racket at approx. 90 degrees to forearm over a 30-metre course with two complete about-turns. Eight stakes are placed in a straight line at 3-metre intervals, with 4½ metres clear at each end of the stakes. Pass successive stakes on different sides (you must sidestep or swerve around them). At the 30-metre mark prop with both feet level and, starting with knees well bent, turn using your hips and pass each stake on the opposite side on the way back. Each of the 30-metre turns must be made in a different direction (clockwise or anti-clockwise).

Sixth Week

Day	Daily Schedule		Distance in Metres	Time* A	B	Relief between Repetitions*
1	Bracket 1.	1 run	2,400	10.40	11.35	7.00 R
	" 2.	8 runs	90 slalom	easy	easy	1.00 R
2	Bracket 1.	2 runs	800	3.00	3.15	3.30 R
	" 2.	8 runs	50	0.07	0.08	0.30 R
	" 3.	8 runs	90 slalom	½ speed		1.00 R
3	Bracket 1.	4 runs	200	0.35	0.37	1.50 W
	" 2.	8 runs	100	0.17	0.18	0.55 R
	" 3.	5 runs	20	full speed from starting blocks (walk back and repeat)		R
	" 4.	10 runs	90 slalom	½ speed		1.00 R
4	Bracket 1.	2 runs	600	2.10	2.25	3.00 W
	" 2.	2 runs	200	0.35	0.37	1.50 W
	" 3.	6 runs	20	full speed S/Bs (walk back and repeat)		R
	" 4.	6 runs	20	full speed S/Bs (walk back and repeat)		R
	" 5.	10 runs	90 slalom	½ speed		1.00 R
5	Bracket 1.	1 run	400	1.20	1.27	2.45 W
	" 2.	10 runs	90 slalom	¾ speed		1.00 R
	" 3.	15 minutes continuous playing with partner without ball on approx. court size				3.00 R
	" 4.	10 minutes each Phantom Squash on approx. court size, each rally of approx. 10 strokes – continuous				3.00 R

Note: If you do not have a partner for Phantom Squash and 15 minutes of playing without the ball, substitute 20 minutes of continuous, meticulous shadow-sparring with 4-second intervals between rallies.

Seventh Week

Day	Daily Schedule		Distance in Metres	Time* A	B	Relief between Repetitions*
1	Bracket 1.	3 runs	600	2.08	2.23	3.00 W
	" 2.	6 runs	100	0.16	0.17	0.50 R
	" 3.	6 runs	20	full speed S/Bs (walk back and repeat)		R
	" 4.	6 runs	20	full speed S/Bs (walk back and repeat)		R
	" 5.	6 runs	90 slalom	full and ¾ speed		1.00 R
	" 6.	6 runs	90 slalom	full and ¾ speed		1.00 R

Note: Where slalom is at full and ¾ speed, make the two complete about-turns and the centre lap at full speed and the remainder at ¾ speed.

Day	Daily Schedule		Distance in Metres	Time* A	B	Relief between Repetitions*
2	Bracket 1.	2 runs	600	2.08	2.23	3.00 W
	" 2.	4 runs	200	0.35	0.37	1.50 W
	" 3.	6 runs	20	full speed S/Bs (walk back and repeat)		R
	" 4.	6 runs	20	full speed S/Bs (walk back and repeat)		R
	" 5.	6 runs	90 slalom	full and ¾ speed		1.00 R
	" 6.	6 runs	90 slalom	full and ¾ speed		1.00 R

* Minutes and seconds

Day	Daily Schedule			Distance in Metres	Time* A	Time* B	Relief between Repetitions*
3	Bracket	1.	4 runs	200	0.35	0.37	1.50 W
	"	2.	4 runs	200	0.35	0.37	1.50 W
	"	3.	6 runs	20	full speed S/Bs (walk back and repeat)		R
	"	4.	6 runs	20	full speed S/Bs (walk back and repeat)		R
	"	5.	6 runs	90 slalom	full and ¾ speed		1.00 R
	"	6.	6 runs	90 slalom	full and ¾ speed		1.00 R
	"	7.	10 minutes each Phantom Squash, each rally of approx. 10 strokes – continuous				3.00 R
4	Bracket	1.	8 runs	100	0.16	0.17	0.50 R
	"	2.	8 runs	100	0.16	0.17	0.50 R
	"	3.	6 runs	20	full speed S/Bs (walk back and repeat)		R
	"	4.	6 runs	20	full speed S/Bs (walk back and repeat)		R
	"	5.	6 runs	90 slalom	full and ¾ speed		1.00 R
	"	6.	6 runs	90 slalom	full and ¾ speed		1.00 R
	"	7.	10 minutes each Phantom Squash, each rally of approx. 10 strokes – continuous				3.00 R
5	Bracket	1.	1 run	400	1.18	1.25	2.45 W
	"	2.	6 runs	90 slalom	full and ¾ speed		1.00 R
	"	3.	6 runs	90 slalom	full and ¾ speed		1.00 R
	"	4.	15 minutes continuous playing with partner without ball on approx. court size				3.00 R
	"	5.	10 minutes each Phantom Squash, each rally of approx. 10 strokes – continuous				3.00 R

Eighth Week

Day	Daily Schedule			Distance in Metres	Time* A	Time* B	Relief between Repetitions*
1	Bracket	1.	3 runs	600	2.05	2.20	3.00 W
	"	2.	6 runs	100	0.16	0.17	0.50 R
	"	3.	6 runs	20	full speed S/Bs (walk back and repeat)		R
	"	4.	6 runs	20	full speed S/Bs (walk back and repeat)		R
	"	5.	6 runs	90 slalom	full and ¾ speed		1.00 R
	"	6.	6 runs	90 slalom	full and ¾ speed		1.00 R
2	Bracket	1.	2 runs	600	2.05	2.20	3.00 W
	"	2.	4 runs	200	0.35	0.37	1.50 W
	"	3.	6 runs	20	full speed S/Bs (walk back and repeat)		R
	"	4.	6 runs	20	full speed S/Bs (walk back and repeat)		R
	"	5.	6 runs	90 slalom	full and ¾ speed		1.00 R
	"	6.	6 runs	90 slalom	full and ¾ speed		1.00 R
3	Bracket	1.	4 runs	200	0.34	0.36	1.50 W
	"	2.	4 runs	200	0.34	0.36	1.50 W
	"	3.	6 runs	20	full speed S/Bs (walk back and repeat)		R
	"	4.	6 runs	20	full speed S/Bs (walk back and repeat)		R
	"	5.	6 runs	90 slalom	full and ¾ speed		1.00 R
	"	6.	6 runs	90 slalom	full and ¾ speed		1.00 R
	"	7.	10 minutes each Phantom Squash, each rally of approx. 10 strokes – continuous				3.00 R
4	Bracket	1.	8 runs	100	0.16	0.17	0.50 R
	"	2.	8 runs	100	0.16	0.17	0.50 R
	"	3.	6 runs	20	full speed S/Bs (walk back and repeat)		R
	"	4.	6 runs	20	full speed S/Bs (walk back and repeat)		R
	"	5.	6 runs	90 slalom	full and ¾ speed		1.00 R
	"	6.	6 runs	90 slalom	full and ¾ speed		1.00 R
	"	7.	10 minutes each Phantom Squash, each rally of approx. 10 strokes – continuous				3.00 R
5	Bracket	1.	1 run	400	1.17	1.24	2.45 W
	"	2.	6 runs	90 slalom	full and ¾ speed		1.00 R
	"	3.	6 runs	90 slalom	full and ¾ speed		1.00 R
	"	4.	15 minutes continuous playing without ball				3.00 R
	"	5.	10 minutes each Phantom Squash, each rally of approx. 10 strokes – continuous				3.00 R

* Minutes and seconds

MALE AND FEMALE SQUASH INTERVAL TRAINING PROGRAM

Ninth to Thirteenth Weeks

During these weeks the actual squash playing program should be greatly increased and the general conditioning program reduced.

To take the greatest advantage of general conditioning early in the season it is preferable to continue during this period with an off-the-court program of three days a week, dropping to two days only in special cases. Research has shown a substantial increase in aerobic (oxygen) capacity from ITP in this period.

The weekly program recommended for this period is as for days two, three and four of the eighth week.

Fourteenth and Subsequent Weeks

You should not have less than five days of general conditioning and squash playing at any time during the season. After the thirteenth week the full general conditioning program should not occupy more than one of those days. Preferably the general conditioning should be additional to the five days of squash playing, but this is an individual matter.

1. One day a week only:

Schedule		Distance in Metres	Time* A	B	Relief between Repetitions*
Bracket 1.	3 runs	800	2.15	2.35	3.00 R
" 2.	4 runs	200	0.28	0.32	1.40 W
" 3.	6 runs	20	full speed from S/Bs (walk back and repeat)		R
" 4.	6 runs	20	full speed from S/Bs (walk back and repeat)		R
" 5.	6 runs	90 slalom	full and ¾ speed		1.00 R
" 6.	6 runs	90 slalom	full and ¾ speed		1.00 R
Females					
Bracket 1.	2 runs	600	2.05	2.20	3.00 W
" 2.	4 runs	200	0.34	0.36	1.50 W
" 3.	6 runs	20	full speed from S/Bs (walk back and repeat)		R
" 4.	6 runs	20	full speed from S/Bs (walk back and repeat)		R
" 5.	6 runs	90 slalom	full and ¾ speed		1.00 R
" 6.	6 runs	90 slalom	full and ¾ speed		1.00 R

* Minutes and seconds

With four or more squash court sessions a week this program should be sufficient to maintain the benefit of your pre-season training. Although the important training is actually playing squash, a day's training out-of-doors on a strict interval basis should stimulate your program and help maintain the three energy capacities built up during the first 13 weeks. However, if you are genuinely seeking to be a champion you should play squash as many times a week as your mental and physical capacities permit. The only limitations are: do not play "tired" squash and guard against staleness.

2. Every day:
   (a) 5-BX (males) or X-BX (females) exercises or exercises individually prescribed.
   (b) Interval skipping. Substitute this for the last (running or skipping) exercise in 5-BX or X-BX and work up to about 10 minutes brisk skipping with 3-second intervals per 30 seconds, i.e. 27 seconds skipping plus 3 seconds rest. Move the feet about while skipping.

On-the-court training

You should start your on-the-court training in week 4 of your program. The first two weeks should be entirely devoted to routines 1 to 6 inclusive of the Practice Routines on page 62. At this time all effort should be devoted to precise stroking and feet positioning and it is preferable to use the horizontal swing in all shots (amend routine 2). Continuous physical effort should be kept to a minimum and as little as two visits to the court a week will be sufficient.

Weeks 6, 7 and 8 should include all exercises in the Practice Routines and also the first stage of the Practice Routines for Controlling the Game from the Centre of the Court on page 70. All strokes should commence with the racket vertical and, except with drop shots and drop shot practice, a full wide-arc swing should be used. Two games a week should be enough, but don't hesitate to play a third if you find it easy and enjoyable. Remember to watch the ball.

Weeks 9-13 should continue with the same practice basis as the previous three weeks, but the second stage of the Practice Routines for Controlling the Game from the Centre of the Court should be substituted for the first stage. During this time you will need three games a week including one for match play. All practice must be directed towards stroke play, feet placement and court movement—and, of course, watching the ball.

By the fourteenth week you will have completed your heavy off-the-court training routine and should now concentrate on all matters relating to court movement, stroke play, basic game, match play and reading the game. Re-read the chapters covering these points to brush up your technical knowledge. Phantom squash, playing without the ball, stroke practice routines and open discussion with fellow players and competitors after matches are all necessary in addition to on-the-court games. Never play lazy squash, and remember to *always watch the ball*.

In practising, you may find it best to have a two-minute interval every 15 minutes, reducing this over the course of four weeks to one-minute intervals, but keep up the same speed of movement. If necessary take even longer intervals to ensure that play always moves at a fast speed.

Be careful to detect when, over a period, your practice and training are having the opposite effect to that expected. If you feel jaded—slow to move, not watching the ball, look tired in the eyes and feel tired in the muscles, and in general have lost your zest—get away from the court completely. Rest up and do no more than light walking until you feel your energy returning. You will not lose your condition quickly.

Your preparation for a championship or very important match requires hard work leading to an exhausting match one week before the event and is associated with recommendations regarding diet later in this chapter. This match is followed by lighter but faster work in the ensuing week.

Individuals differ in their capacities but this general advice should form the basis of each individual's final preparation.

NUTRITION

I extend my warmest thanks to Dr Alan Morton of the University of Western Australia from whose paper "Nutrition of the Athlete", presented at the national seminar for sports coaches organised by the Australian Department of Tourism and Recreation and the Australian Sports Council in Melbourne during May 1975, I have extracted directly or in substance the information contained in this section. (For the full paper see Sports Coaching, *Australian Government Publishing Service, Canberra 1976.)*

Sound nutrition is one of the most important factors governing a good performance in squash. Optimum nutrition does not replace the need for good training, but is an additive needed to obtain maximum performance.

The basic principles of your training diet are:
1. Your diet does not differ from that of a sedentary person other than in the amount of food intake required.
2. If you eat a balanced diet and the caloric intake is enough to balance the caloric output, food supplements will not be necessary.
3. Your diet should be palatable.
4. Although the pre-game meal is important, performance will depend more on the diet over the rest of the week.
5. You must maintain adequate hydration by drinking, up to and even during the match, especially in a hot or humid climate.
6. Performance in endurance events such as squash can be improved by specific dietary regimes which involve high carbohydrate intake.
7. Glycogen (animal starch found in the liver and muscles) stockpiling provides additional glycogen for fuel plus reserve water (metabolic water).

Daily food requirements

The required nutrients can be divided into six classifications. These are:
1. Carbohydrates: sugars and starches. Rich

sources include cereal grains (and flour), potatoes, rice, spaghetti, sugar, honey, sweet fruits and milk.

2. Fats: occur in liquid form (as oil) and solid form.
3. Proteins: meat, fish, poultry, cheese, eggs.
4. Vitamins: different types occur in varying amounts in all foods. If well balanced meals are eaten there will be no deficiency of vitamins, and consequently there will be no need to include vitamin supplements in the athlete's diet.
5. Minerals: present in milk, meat, vegetables, fruit, etc.
6. Water: about two-thirds of your weight is water.

The amount of food required each day has been a long and hotly debated subject. Dr Morton says:

The amount of food intake required each day depends on the activity level of the individual. The more active, the more calories expended, thus the more calories that must be ingested to maintain body weight. However, it has been suggested that a minimum of about 2,500 kilocalories must be taken in each day to provide the minimum nutritional requirements.

This minimum can best be met by following the pattern outlined below:

Table 8

Minimum Daily food lineup[2]
(approximately 2,500 calories)

Food group	total servings per day
Milk	4 cups
Meat (fish, poultry, cheese or eggs)	140g (5oz) of edible meat without bone or fat
Dark green or deep yellow vegetables	1 serving (½ cup)
Citrus fruits	1 serving (½ cup)
Other fruits and vegetables	2 servings (1 cup)
Bread (enriched or whole grain bread, cereal or potatoes)	13 servings
Fats (butter, margarine or other fat spreads)	10 servings (10 teaspoons)

Because of the differences which exist between individual likes and dislikes, and even enzyme systems, it is difficult to establish one dietary pattern which will be optimal for all. A useful guide is that used by de Vries,[14] which suggests that 48 per cent, 40 per cent and 12 per cent of the total daily calories should be provided by carbohydrate, fat and protein respectively.

Research has indicated that the mature athlete will not need more protein than the sedentary individual (i.e. 1 gram of protein per kilogram of body weight per day). There may be a need for an increased intake during that part of the training period when muscle mass and other tissue (particularly blood protein) is being increased [during the three-month pre-season stamina build up], but certainly 2 grams of protein per kilogram of body weight per day will be more than adequate. This conclusion is based on the fact that there is very little

increase in the amount of nitrogen excreted in the urine with increase in exercise levels. A higher protein intake will be required also if the athlete is young and still growing. When the additional protein is required the proportion of carbohydrate, fat and protein should be approximately 48 per cent, 32 per cent and 20 per cent respectively.

Although the diet must contain adequate amounts of the various required nutrients there is no evidence to suggest that supernormal intakes of these nutrients will increase physical performance ability. Deficiency in vitamin intake will lower the physical performance capacity and it appears that the lack of the B vitamins shows performance decrement more quickly. This is probably due to the part they play in the metabolic pathways.

Dr Morton believes good nutrition plays an important part in achieving optimum physical performance:

In this continual effort to attain athletic excellence, the emphasis placed on the importance of proper diets for athletes has been considerable and can be credited as important to athletic success. Although there may be general agreement that an athlete must have a good diet in order to perform at his best there is far from general agreement about what constitutes such a good diet. Much has been written about this subject, and the views expressed have differed so vehemently that the athletes and coaches are faced with a mass of conflicting information. These differences have reached a state where the subject of special foods and diets has become the centre of many idiosyncrasies which are still associated with the training for athletics[26].

In 1960 Mayer and Bullen[23] claimed that "the concept that any well-balanced diet is all that athletes actually require for peak performance has not been superseded." Today most work physiologists and nutritionists agree that there is still no evidence to suggest that an athlete will require different foods to the sedentary individual, except that he will need a greater intake of food to provide adequate calories. This is shown in a statement by Shephard[23] in 1973:

There is no sound evidence that the physiological powers of a person in sound health are improved by a departure from a normal well-balanced, mixed diet. This should be palatable, and provide an adequate intake of calories, with a reasonable balance of protein, fat and carbohydrate and no more than the natural content of vitamins and minerals.

Despite this belief, however, significant evidence is given subsequently in the paper that benefit can be gained by special attention to diet in the week before an important match. If you plan to play weekly competition matches you should study the following information and apply whatever parts of it specifically relate to you.

The duration of work and the metabolic mixture

Many experiments have been conducted on athletes performing similar endurance exercises on firstly a normal mixed diet and secondly a high carbohydrate diet. The results of these experiments show that the carbohydrate diet (which produces the higher level of muscle glycogen) does not enable the athlete to run faster at the beginning of a race but does allow him to maintain the pace for a longer period of time. An interesting experiment showed that in a game of soccer those players having high initial glycogen levels covered greater distances in each half of the game and spent a lesser percentage of the time walking than did those with low initial levels.

It appears that it is important to have a high initial muscle glycogen level in events lasting 40 minutes or more. As a hard and even squash match would be in the region of 60-90 minutes (and could be longer), it is particularly important to pay attention to this aspect of diet.

Diet the week before an important event

The following program will provide a high storage of glycogen prior to an event:

1. **Day 7 before the match:** play squash until you reach the point of exhaustion.
2. **Days 6-4 before the match:** follow a high energy-low carbohydrate diet (which keeps glycogen level low):
   Breakfast
   ½ grapefruit or ½ cup grapefruit juice
   2 eggs
   generous serving bacon, ham or sausages
   butter or margarine as desired
   1 thin slice whole wheat bread
   1 cup milk or half milk and half water
   Lunch and dinner
   clear bouillon or ½ cup tomato juice
   large serving fish, poultry or liver (more than 170g–6oz)
   mixed green salad or 1 cup cooked green vegetables
   salad dressing, butter or margarine as desired
   1 cup milk or half milk and half water
   artificially sweetened jelly with whipped cream (no sugar)
   Snacks
   cheddar cheese
   nuts
   1 slice whole grain bread
   artificially sweetened lemonade
3. **Days 3-1 before the match:** follow a very high energy-high carbohydrate diet (which quickly and substantially builds up glycogen level):
   Breakfast
   1 cup orange or pineapple juice
   hot cereal as desired
   eggs and/or pikelets or drop scones
   generous serving bacon, ham or sausages
   butter or margarine as desired
   2-4 slices whole grain bread
   chocolate drink or cocoa as desired
   Lunch and dinner
   cream or legume soup or chowder
   large serving fish, poultry or liver (more than 170g–6oz)
   beans or fruit
   salad dressing butter or margarine as desired
   1 cup milk or half milk and half water or milkshake
   2-4 slices whole grain bread rolls, or potato
   sweet pie, cake, pudding or ice-cream
   Snacks
   fruit, especially dates, raisins, apples, bananas
   milk or milkshakes
   biscuits or confectionary

Dr Morton warns that while this regime to stockpile glycogen is advantageous for endurance athletes (in events lasting at least 40 minutes) it is detrimental to sportsmen in short-term events. This is especially true if the athlete is required to lift or support his own body weight as each gram of carbohydrate requires 2.7 grams of water to be bound to it for storage. This could mean about 2-3 litres (4-5 pints) of water bound to glycogen, thus increasing the body weight by 2-3 kg (4½-6½ lbs). It may also develop the feeling of heaviness and stiffness.

He also points out that a limitation of the stockpiling technique is that it can only be accomplished infrequently, i.e. no more than once every three or four weeks. Therefore sportsmen who have to perform at their top each week are advised to live on a high carbohydrate diet for the last three days of each week to ensure the maximum weekly glycogen level and then the stockpiling regime can be used prior to international matches or finals.

As far as weekly matches are concerned, you will have to determine for yourself whether or not a departure from your normal well balanced diet is necessary other than for special matches, i.e. where every advantage in endurance may be necessary.

For a championship tournament the seven-day program to provide "glycogen overshoot" should commence (i.e. the "game to exhaustion" takes place) seven days before the first round. As the timing of the "overshoot" can not be as accurate as for a single match, you should commence the tournament with a maximum "overshoot" and endeavour to maintain it throughout the tournament by following a high carbohydrate diet. The success of this will largely depend on the ease or difficulty of your passage through the early rounds, but at worst you will be well prepared for your first tough encounter and rely mainly on daily replenishment from the high carbohydrate diet for your glycogen store for later matches.

It is also important that any exercise taken as from six days prior to the tournament, apart from matches played, is light, sharp playing exercise with adequate rest intervals. More than usual rest should be taken in general non-exercise time.

The pre-game meal

Although your performance will depend as much, or more, on the meals throughout the week as it will on the pre-game meal, this meal is still very important prior to important matches.

Extensive evidence shows that if an athlete is preparing for an activity which requires vigorous and sustained muscular activity he should ensure that his muscles and liver have an abundant supply of carbohydrates. It appears, also, that the meal which is followed by the greatest increase in blood sugar level is the best meal to eat prior to an endurance-type event.

The old-time pre-game meal of steak has been tested in relation to a high carbohydrate liquid meal and all scientific evidence shows that the latter is clearly superior. The recommendation, therefore, is that the pre-game meal be a high carbohydrate liquid meal and not a high protein meal. As it seems that a high carbohydrate liquid meal generally passes through the stomach in less than two hours it would be best to have this meal two hours before the event.

Dr Morton also recommends that you pay attention to your post-game meal, off-season diet and fluid intake:

The post-game meal

Most athletes do not feel like eating soon after the event, but a period of rest and relaxation will result in the appetite returning more quickly. This is because it takes some time for the body to revert back to its readiness to digest food after vigorous activity.

Most will be prepared to take fluid after the event. This should be encouraged as the body's fluid stores will need to be replenished.

The post-game meal can be any palatable, good sized, balanced meal.

Off-season diet

One of the biggest problems facing a coach at the beginning of the season is the degree of obesity that many of his athletes exhibit. This means that much of the early training is aimed at weight reduction and therefore delays the onset of the coach's program.

The reasons for this overweight is simple mathematics. In the off-season the calorie expenditure is greatly reduced due to the cessation of hard training; however, many do not reduce the food intake. Thus the excess calories are converted to fat and stored.

Athletes must reduce food intakes to balance the decreased energy expenditure of the off-season period.

Fluid intake

One of the most dangerous pre-game practices is that of "drying out" for the game. This practice of refraining from drinking is physiologically a very dangerous procedure. This is especially true when the environmental temperature is high and/or the relative humidity is high. This type of environment often occurs in Australia even during early pre-season training, and during the trial games for winter sports such as football, for example. Temperatures in the 30-35 deg C (86-95 deg F) range, plus high humidity, may also be encountered when teams tour countries in the tropics.

The danger exists because under high temperature and/or high humidity the sweat loss required to try to dissipate the body heat accumulating, due to increased metabolism and due to the environmental heat, can lead to excessive loss of body water. Drying out further aggravates this situation.

The sweat loss may be as high as 3.5 litres (about 6 pints) per hour, resulting in a weight loss (fluid) of 4.5-6 kg (10-14 lb) in a football game or training session. This loss of body water greatly increases the demands placed on the circulatory system and the body's sweating mechanism. It can lead to heat cramps, heat exhaustion, heat stroke and death. In one three-year period in the USA, twelve footballers of high school or college level died due to the effects of dehydration.[15]

It is ridiculous to expect the athlete to maintain maximum efficiency of performance while losing fluid in a lengthy event and not replacing it until the game is over. Surely it is more advisable to restore fluid losses a little at a time during the contest, if this is possible. Research has shown that even after a fluid loss equal to as little as 1 per cent of body weight there is a reduction in physical work capacity. Where fluid loss equals about 4-5 per cent of the body weight, the athlete can expect a 20-30 per cent reduction in his capacity for heavy work[27].

The replacement of lost water is subject to a few general rules. These are:
(a) the drink should not be excessively cold; icy-cold water can cause contractions in the muscles of the wall of the stomach causing cramp and pain (suggest 12-16 deg C—54-61 deg F);

(b) the drink ought not to be fizzy or gaseous; this produces distensions and again, feelings of discomfort;

(c) drinks should not be taken in excessive quantities during the event. The motto should be "little and often". It is recommended that if 100-300 ml is ingested every 10-15 minutes a total uptake of 1-1.5 litres (about 2-3 pints) of fluid can be accomplished per hour. Fifty to 60 grams of glucose can also be taken in this time if the fluid contains 5-10 per cent glucose[27].

Salt, too, is lost in the sweat. When you sweat profusely you shed a great deal of salt. For every kilogram of fluid weight lost, 1 litre of fluid and 2 grams of salt are lost. Salt must be kept in balance in the body in much the same way as fluid.

The best replacement fluid is one that is isotonic to sweat, i.e. contains about 1-2 grams of salt per litre of fluid. Tomato juice apparently meets this requirement, as do some of the commercially prepared products such as Staminade, Vigorade and Gatorade, and the following formula:

2 grams of salt
1 litre (2 pints) of water
the juice of one or two lemons or some
    artificial flavouring (to mask the salty taste)
50-100 grams of glucose (not more than 100 grams)

However, salt replacement is of secondary importance to fluid replacement, and is not required during the event unless very heavy sweat losses have occurred.

Applying the above principles to squash in normal winter conditions we reach the following conclusions:

1. Don't "dry-out" for a match.
2. When playing a match and sweating becomes profuse, drink a few mouthfuls of slightly warmed water or replacement fluid after each hard game.
3. Take adequate replacement fluid after a match involving heavy sweat loss. When sweating is excessive have some salt replacement.

Finally, always remember that thirst is usually not a good guide to the body's fluid need, as it is quenched before adequate fluid has been ingested, therefore forced drinking is usually required.

THE RULES

The official rules of the Singles Game of Squash Rackets (soft-ball) are those approved by the International Squash Rackets Federation (ISRF).

As in all games, the rules of Squash have been designed to help everyone achieve maximum enjoyment and fair treatment. Study them well and be sure you always adhere to the principles and details embodied in them.

The following are the current official rules for the Singles Game of Squash Rackets as amended 1 January 1978:

1. The Game, How Played. The game of Squash Rackets is played between two players with standard rackets, with balls officially approved by ISRF and in a rectangular court of standard dimensions, enclosed on all four sides.

2. The Score. A match shall consist of the best of three or five games at the option of the promoters of the competition. Each game is 9 points up; that is to say, the player who first wins 9 points wins the game, except that, on the score being called 8-all for the first time, Hand-out may choose, before the next service is delivered, to continue the game to 10, in which case the player, who first scores two more points, wins the game. Hand-out must in either case clearly indicate his choice to the Marker, if any, and to his opponent.
Note to Referees. If Hand-out does not make clear his choice before the next service, the Referee shall stop play and require him to do so.

3. Points, How Scored. Points can only be scored by Hand-in. When a player fails to serve or to make a good return in accordance with the Rules, the opponent wins the stroke. When Hand-in wins the stroke, he scores a point; when Hand-out wins a stroke, he becomes Hand-in.

4. The Right to Serve. The right to serve first is decided by the spin of a racket. Thereafter the server continues to serve until he loses a stroke, when his opponent becomes the server, and so on throughout the match.

5. Service. The ball before being struck shall be dropped or thrown in the air and shall not touch the walls or floor. The ball shall be served direct on to the front wall, so that on its return, unless volleyed, it would fall to the floor within the back quarter of the court opposite to the server's box from which the service has been delivered.

At the beginning of each game and of each hand, the server may serve from either box, but after scoring a point he shall then serve from the other, and so on alternately as long as he remains Hand-in or until the end of the game. If the server serves from the wrong box, there shall be no penalty and the service shall count as if served from the correct box, except that Hand-out may, if he does not attempt to take the service, demand that it be served from the other box.

A player with the use of only one arm may utilise his racket to project the ball into the air.

6. Good Service. A service is good which is not a fault or which does not result in the server serving his hand-out in accordance with Rule 9. If the server serves one fault, he shall serve again.

7. Fault. A service is a fault (unless the server serves his hand-out under Rule 9):

(a) If the server fails to stand with at least one foot on the floor within, and not touching the line surrounding the service box at the moment of striking the ball (called a foot-fault).
(b) If the ball is served on to, or below, the cut line.
(c) If the ball served first touches the floor on, or in front of, the short line or on or outside the half court line.

8. Fault, If Taken. Hand-out may take a fault. If he attempts to do so, the service thereupon becomes good and the ball continues in play. If he does not attempt to do so, the ball shall cease to be in play, provided that, if the ball, before it bounces twice upon the floor, touches the server or anything he wears or carries, the server shall lose the stroke.

9. Serving Hand-out. The server serves his hand-out and loses the stroke:

(a) If the ball is served on to, or below, the board, or out, or against any part of the court before the front wall.
(b) If the ball is not dropped or thrown in the air, or touches the wall or floor before being struck, or if he fails to strike the ball, or strikes it more than once.
(c) If he serves two consecutive faults.
(d) If the ball, before it has bounced twice upon the floor, or has been struck by his opponent, touches the server or anything he wears or carries.

10. Let. A let is an undecided stroke, and the service or rally, in respect of which a let is allowed, shall not count and the server shall serve again from the same box. A let shall not annul a previous fault.

Note to Referees: This last sentence applies only to a second or subsequent service after a fault has not been taken.

11. The Play. After a good service has been delivered, the players return the ball alternately until one or other fails to make a good return, or the ball otherwise ceases to be in play in accordance with the Rules.

12. Good Return. A return is good if the ball, before it has bounced twice upon the floor, is returned by the striker on to the front wall above the board, without touching the floor or any part of the striker's body or clothing, provided the ball is not hit twice or out.
Note to Referees. It shall not be considered a good

return if the ball touches the board before or after it hits the front wall.

13. Strokes, How Won. A player wins a stroke:

(a) Under Rule 9.
(b) If the opponent fails to make a good return of the ball in play.
(c) If the ball in play touches his opponent or anything he wears or carries, except as is otherwise provided by Rules 14 and 15.
(d) If a stroke is awarded by the Referee as provided for in the Rules.

14. Hitting an Opponent with the Ball. If an otherwise good return of the ball has been made, but before reaching the front wall it hits the striker's opponent, or his racket, or anything he wears or carries, then:

(a) If the ball would have made a good return, and would have struck the front wall without first touching any other wall, the striker shall win the stroke, except that, if the striker shall have followed the ball round, and so turned, before playing the ball, a let shall be allowed.
(b) If the ball would otherwise have made a good return, a let shall be allowed unless, in the Referee's opinion, a winning stroke has been intercepted, then the striker shall win the stroke.
(c) If the ball would not have made a good return, the striker shall lose the stroke. The ball shall cease to be in play, even if it subsequently goes up.

15. Further Attempts to Hit the Ball. If the striker strikes at, and misses the ball, he may make further attempts to return it. If, after being missed, the ball touches his opponent, or his racket, or anything he wears or carries, then:

(a) If the striker would otherwise have made a good return, a let shall be allowed.
(b) If the striker could not have made a good return, he loses the stroke.

If any such further attempt is successful, but the ball, before reaching the front wall, hits the striker's opponent, or his racket, or anything he wears or carries, a let shall be allowed, and Rule 14(a) shall not apply.

16. Appeals:

(a) An appeal may be made against any decision of the Marker, except for (b) (i) below.
(b) (i) No appeal shall be made in respect of the Marker's call of "Foot fault" or "Fault" to the first service.
(ii) If the Marker calls "Foot fault" or "Fault"

to the second service, the server may appeal, and if the decision is reversed, a let shall be allowed.

   (iii) If the Marker allows the second service, Hand-out may appeal, either immediately, or at the end of the rally, if he has played the ball, and if the decision is reversed, Hand-in becomes Hand-out.

   (iv) If the Marker does not call "Foot fault" or "Fault" to the first service, Hand-out may appeal that the service was a foot fault or fault, provided he makes no attempt to play the ball. If the Marker does not call "Out" or "Not up" to the first service, Hand-out may appeal, either immediately or at the end of the rally, if he has played the ball. In either case, if the appeal is disallowed, Hand-out shall lose the stroke.

(c) An appeal under Rule 12 shall be made at the end of the rally.

(d) In all cases where a let is desired an appeal shall be made to the Referee with the words "let, please". Play shall thereupon cease until the Referee has given his decision.

(e) No appeal may be made after the delivery of a service for anything that occurred before that service was delivered.

17. Fair View and Freedom to Play the Ball:

(a) After playing a ball, a player must make every effort to get out of his opponent's way. That is:

   (i) A player must make every effort to give his opponent a fair view of the ball, so that he may sight it adequately for the purpose of playing it.

   (ii) A player must make every effort not to interfere with, or crowd, his opponent in the latter's attempt to get to, or play, the ball.

   (iii) A player must make every effort to allow his opponent, as far as the latter's position permits, freedom to play the ball directly to the front wall, or side walls near the front wall.

(b) If any such form of interference has occurred, and, in the opinion of the Referee, the player has not made every effort to avoid causing it, the Referee shall on appeal, or stopping play without waiting for an appeal, award the stroke to his opponent.

(c) However, if interference has occurred, but in the opinion of the Referee the player has made every effort to avoid causing it, the Referee shall on appeal or stopping play without waiting for an appeal, award a let, except that if his opponent is prevented from making a

winning return by such interference or by distraction from the player, the Referee shall award the stroke to the opponent.

(d) When, in the opinion of the Referee, a player refrains from playing the ball, which, if played, would clearly and undoubtedly have won the rally under the terms of Rule 14(a) or (b), he shall be awarded the stroke.

Notes to Referees:

(i) The practice of impeding an opponent in his efforts to play the ball by crowding or obscuring his view, is highly detrimental to the game, and Referees should have no hesitation in enforcing paragraph (b) above.

(ii) The words "interfere with" in (a)(ii) above must be interpreted to include the case of a player having to wait for an excessive swing of his opponent's racket.

18. Let, When Allowed.
Notwithstanding anything contained in these Rules, and provided always that the striker could have made a good return:

(a) A let may be allowed:

   (i) If, owing to the position of the striker, his opponent is unable to avoid being touched by the ball before the return is made.
   Note to Referees. This rule shall be construed to include the cases of the striker, whose position in front of his opponent makes it impossible for the latter to see the ball, or who shapes as if to play the ball and changes his mind at the last moment, preferring to take the ball off the back wall, the ball in either case hitting his opponent, who is between the striker and the back wall. This is not, however, to be taken as conflicting in any way with the Referee's duties under Rule 17.

   (ii) If the ball in play touches any articles lying in the court.

   (iii) If the striker refrains from hitting the ball owing to a reasonable fear of injuring his opponent.

   (iv) If the striker, in the act of playing the ball, touches his opponent.

   (v) If the Referee is asked to decide an appeal and is unable to do so.

   (vi) If a player drops his racket, calls out or in any other way distracts his opponent, and the Referee considers that such occurrence has caused the opponent to lose the stroke.

(b) A Let shall be allowed:

   (i) If Hand-out is not ready and does not attempt to take the service.

   (ii) If a ball breaks during play.

(iii) If an otherwise good return has been made, but the ball goes out of court on its first bounce.

(iv) As provided for in Rules 14, 15, 16(b)(iii), 23 and 24.

(c) No let shall be allowed when a player has made an attempt to play the ball except as provided for under Rules 15, 18(a)(iv), 18(b)(ii) and 18(b)(iii).

(d) Unless an appeal is made by one of the players, no let shall be allowed except where these Rules definitely provide for a let, namely Rules 14(a) and (b), 17 and 18(b)(ii) and (iii).

19. New Ball. At any time, when the ball is not in actual play, a new ball may be substituted by mutual consent of the players, or, on appeal by either player, at the discretion of the Referee.

20. Knock-up:

(a) The Referee shall allow on the court of play a period not exceeding five minutes to the two players together for the purpose of knocking up, or in the event of the players electing to knock up separately, the Referee shall allow the first player a period of three and a half minutes and to his opponent, two and a half minutes. In the event of a separate knock-up, the choice of knocking-up first shall be decided by the spin of a racket. The Referee shall allow a further period for the players to warm the ball up if the match is being resumed after a considerable delay.

(b) Where a new ball has been substituted under Rule 18(b)(ii) or 19, the Referee shall allow the ball to be knocked-up to playing conditions. Play shall resume on the direction of the Referee, or prior mutual consent of the players.

(c) Between games the ball shall remain on the floor of the court in view and knocking-up shall not be permitted except by mutual consent of the players.

21. Play in a Match is to be Continuous. After the first service is delivered, play shall be continuous so far as is practical, provided that:

(a) At any time play may be suspended owing to bad light or other circumstances beyond the control of the players, for such period as the Referee shall decide. In the event of play being suspended for the day, the match shall start afresh, unless both players agree to the contrary.

(b) The Referee shall award a game to the opponent of any player, who, in his opinion, persists, after due warning, in delaying the play in order to recover his strength or wind, or for any other reason.

(c) An interval of one minute shall be permitted between games and of two minutes between the fourth and fifth games of a five-game match. A player may leave the court during such intervals, but shall be ready to resume play at the end of the stated time. When 10 seconds of the interval permitted between games are left, the Marker shall call "10 seconds" to warn the players to be ready to resume play. Should either player fail to do so when required by the Referee, a game may be awarded to his opponent.

(d) In the event of an injury, the Referee may require a player to continue play or concede the match, except where the injury is contributed to by his opponent, or where it was caused by dangerous play on the part of the opponent. In the former case, the Referee may allow time for the injured player to receive attention and recover, and in the latter, the injured player shall be awarded the match under Rule 24(c)(ii).

(e) In the event of a ball breaking, a new ball may be knocked-up, as provided for in Rule 20(b).

Notes to Referees:

(i) In allowing time for a player to receive attention and recover, the Referee should ensure that there is no conflict with the obligation of a player to comply with Rule 21(b), that is, that the effects of the injury are not exaggerated and used as an excuse to recover strength or wind.

(ii) The Referee should not interpret the words "contributed to" by the opponent to include the situation where the injury to the player is a result of that player occupying an unnecessarily close position to his opponent.

22. Control of a Match. A match is normally controlled by a Referee, assisted by a Marker. One person may be appointed to carry out the functions of both Referee and Marker. When a decision has been made by a Referee, he shall announce it to the players and the Marker shall repeat it with the subsequent score.

Up to one hour before the commencement of a match either player may request a Referee and/or a Marker other than appointed, and this request may be considered and a substitute appointed. Players are not permitted to request any such change after the commencement of a match, unless both agree to do so. In either case the decision as to whether an official is to be replaced or not must remain in the hands of the Tournament Referee, where applicable.

23. Duties of Marker:

(a) The Marker calls the play and the score, with the server's score first. He shall call "Foot fault"; "Fault": "Out": "Not up" or "Down" as appropriate.

(b) If in the course of play the Marker calls "Not up" or "Out" or in the case of a second service "Fault" or "Foot fault" then the rally shall cease.

(c) If the Marker's decision is reversed on appeal, a let shall be allowed, except as provided for in Rule 24(b)(iv) and (v)

(d) Any service or return shall be considered good unless otherwise called.

(e) After the server has served a fault, which has not been taken, the Marker shall repeat the score and add the words "One fault", before the server serves again. This call should be repeated should subsequent rallies end in a let, until the point is finally decided.

(f) When no Referee is appointed, the Marker shall exercise all the powers of the Referee.

(g) If the Marker is unsighted or uncertain, he shall call on the Referee to make the relevant decision; if the latter is unable to do so, a let shall be allowed.

24. Duties of Referee:

(a) The Referee shall award Lets and Strokes and make decisions where called for by the Rules, and shall decide all appeals, including those against the Marker's calls and decisions. The decision of the Referee shall be final.

(b) He shall in no way intervene in the Marker's calling except:
  (i) Upon appeal by one of the players.
  (ii) As provided for in Rule 17.
  (iii) When it is evident that the score has been incorrectly called, in which case he should draw the Marker's attention to the fact.
  (iv) When the Marker has failed to call the ball "Not up" or "Out", and on appeal he rules that such was in fact the case, the stroke should be awarded accordingly.
  (v) When the Marker has called "Not up" or "Out", and on appeal he rules that this was not the case, a Let shall be allowed except that if in the Referee's opinion, the Marker's call had interrupted an undoubted winning return, he shall award the stroke accordingly.
  (vi) In exceptional circumstances when he is absolutely convinced that the Marker has made an obvious error in stopping play or allowing play to continue, he shall immediately rule accordingly.

(c) The Referee is responsible that all times laid down in the Rules are strictly adhered to.

(d) In exceptional cases, the Referee may order:
  (i) A player, who has left the court, to play on.
  (ii) A player to leave the court and to award the match to the opponent.
  (iii) A match to be awarded to a player whose opponent fails to be present in court within 10 minutes of the advertised time of play.
  (iv) Play to be stopped in order to warn that the conduct of one or both of the players is leading to an infringement of the Rules. A Referee should avail himself of this Rule as early as possible when either player is showing a tendency to break the provisions of Rule 17.

(e) If after a warning a player continues to contravene Rule 20(c) the Referee shall award a game to the opponent.

25. Colour of Players' Clothing.

For amateur events under the control of the ISRF players are required to wear all white clothing provided however, the ISRF officers at their sole discretion can waive compliance with this Rule.

Member countries of the ISRF may legislate, if they so desire, to allow clothing of a light pastel colour to be worn for all other events under their control.

The Referee's decision thereon to be final.

Note: Footwear is deemed clothing for this Rule.

APPENDIX I: DEFINITIONS

Board or Tin. The expression denoting a band, the top edge of which is 0.483m (19in) from the floor across the lower part of the front wall above which the ball must be returned before the stroke is good.

Cut Line. A line upon the front wall, the top edge of which is 1.829m (6ft) above the floor and extending the full width of the court.

Down. The expression used to indicate that a ball has been struck against the tin or board.

Game Ball. The state of the game when the server requires one point to win is said to be "Game Ball".

Half-court Line. A line set out upon the floor parallel to the side walls, dividing the back half of the court into two equal parts.

Hand-in. The player who serves.

Hand-out. The player who receives the service; also the expression used to indicate that Hand-in has become Hand-out.

Hand. The period from the time when a player becomes Hand-in until he becomes Hand-out.

Match Ball. The state of the match when the server requires one point to win is said to be Match Ball.

Not Up. The expression used to denote that a ball has not been served or returned above the board in accordance with the Rules.

Out. The ball is out when it touches the front, sides or back of the court above the area prepared for play or passes over any cross bars or other part of the roof of the court. The lines delimiting such area, the lighting equipment and the roof are out.

Point. A point is won by the player who is Hand-in and who wins a stroke.

Quarter Court. One part of the back half of the court which has been divided into two equal parts by the half-court line.

Service Box or Box. A delimited area in each quarter court from within which Hand-in services.

Short Line. A line set out upon the floor parallel to and 5.486m (18ft) from the front wall and extending the full width of the court.

Striker. The player whose turn it is to play after the ball has hit the front wall.

Stroke. A stroke is won by the player whose opponent fails to serve or make a good return in accordance with the Rules.

Stop. Expression used by the Referee to stop play.

Time. Expression used by the Referee to start play.

APPENDIX II: DIMENSIONS OF A SINGLES COURT

Length: 9.75m (32ft)

Breadth: 6.40m (21ft)

Height to upper edge of cut line on front wall: 1.83m (6ft)

Height to lower edge of front-wall line: 4.57m (15ft)

Height to lower edge of back-wall line: 2.13m (7ft)

Distance to further edge of short line from front wall: 5.49m (18ft)

Height to upper edge of board from ground: 0.48m (19in)

Thickness of board (flat or rounded at top): 12.5mm to 25mm (½-1in).

Height of side-wall line: The diagonal line joining the front-wall line and the back-wall line.

The service boxes shall be entirely enclosed on three sides within the court by lines, the short line forming the side nearest to the front wall, the side wall bounding the fourth side.

The internal dimensions of the service boxes shall be 1.601m (5ft 3in).

All dimensions in the court shall be measured, where practicable, from the junction of the floor and front wall.

All lines marking the boundaries of the court shall be 50mm (2in) in width and all other lines shall not exceed 50mm (2in) in width. All lines shall be coloured red.

In respect of the outer boundary lines on the walls, it is suggested that the plaster should be so shaped as to produce a concave channel along such lines.

APPENDIX III: DIMENSIONS OF A RACKET

The overall length shall not exceed 685mm (27in). The internal stringing area shall not exceed 215mm (8½in) in length by 184mm (7¼in) in breadth and the framework of the head shall measure not more than 14mm ($^9/_{16}$in) across the face by 20mm ($^{13}/_{16}$in) deep.

The framework of the head shall be of wood. The handle shaft shall be made of wood, cane, metal or glass fibre. The grip and foundation may be made of any suitable material.

APPENDIX IV: SPECIFICATION FOR SQUASH RACKET BALLS

The ball must conform to the following:

1. It must weigh not less than 23.3g and not more than 24.6g (approx 360-380 grains).

2. Its diameter must be not less than 39.5mm and not more than 41.5mm (approx 1.56-1.63in).

3. It must have a surface finish which guarantees continuing correct rebound.

4. It must be of a type specifically approved for championship play by the International Squash Rackets Federation.

5. Compression Specification:

   (i) The ball is mounted in an apparatus and a load of 0.5 kg is applied which deforms the ball slightly. Subsequent deformation in the test is measured from this datum.

   (ii) An additional load of 2.4 kg is applied and this deforms the ball further. The deformation from the datum position is recorded.

   (iii) The deformation obtained in (ii) should be between 3 and 7 mm for balls of playing properties acceptable to the ISRF.

INFORMATION SUPPLEMENTARY TO THE RULES

1. STANDARD CALLS FOR MATCH PLAY

Introduction. This should be made in the following way: "Final of the Open Championship, Smith serving, Jones receiving, best of five games, love all."

Score. The score "1-1" to be called "One all", not "One each", "One-one", etc.

Out, Not up, Down. Calls to be made at end of rally when necessary. When applicable the call of "Not up" to be followed by "Double hit" or "Side wall" (on service) to help the players understand why the shot was wrong.

New Game. After the call of "Time", the Marker shall set the new game in motion by calling the score in games, with the server's games first, followed by the point score, which will be "love all", e.g. "one game to love—love all", etc.

Order of Calls. At the end of a rally the Marker shall make the necessary calls in the following order:

1. Any call which will affect the score: these are "Out", "Not up", "Down", the repetition of any decision by the Referee, e.g. "Yes let", "No let", or "Stroke to Smith", or the call of "Hand out". (*Note*: The Referee should reply to an appeal for a let by saying "Yes let" or "No let" or "Stroke to Smith", not "Point to Smith".)
2. The words of the score itself, e.g. "Eight-two".
3. Any comments on the score, e.g. "Game ball", "Match ball", "One fault", "No set" or "Set two".

2. CONSTRUCTION OF A COURT

The following are the international championship standards for a squash court as set down by the ISRF.

The front wall shall be constructed of concrete, brick or similar material with a near smooth concrete or plaster finish. The side and rear walls to be constructed of similar materials. The rear wall, for viewing purposes, can be constructed of glass or similar materials.

All walls shall be white or near white. The board shall be white or near white in colour and made of some resonant material. The top edge shall be either rounded or flat incorporating a red line to a depth of 50mm (2in) measured from the top.

The floor shall be constructed of light coloured wooden boards which will run lengthwise and not across the court. The floor must be level (horizontal).

The area above the height of play on the back wall (if wall continues upwards) should be constructed of some resonant material.

All lines shall be coloured red.

The minimum clear height above the front wall playing surface to be 1.25m, giving a clear height from the court floor of 5.8m (19ft).

The minimum clear height at 3.5m (approx 12ft) back from the front wall to be 6.4m (21ft) above the floor.

Where a flat ceiling is used the height set at 3.5m back should apply as a minimum.

The ceiling should be white or near white.

LOOKING BEHIND THE RULES

It is a tribute to the original rule-makers and subsequent revisionists that a mere 25 rules cover the whole of the singles game. The majority of them are basic machinery rules, and others have been included to overcome difficulties created by players who have found ways and means of gaining unfair advantage under rules originally designed for simplicity of communication.

Squash can be a difficult game to referee. Experienced players develop an advanced perspective of situations occurring in the heat of matches and should apply this experience in refereeing matches to make known their interpretations to other players for the benefit of the game.

The crux of the rules is Rule 17, "Fair View and Freedom to Play the Ball", which demands keen analysis by every player.

Historically this rule catered for lets only but the now great importance of penalty points makes it a rule under which the outlook and interpretations of the referee could well decide the outcome of a match—an unfortunate circumstance which, I am afraid, has been brought on by players themselves.

The original allowance of lets under Rule 17 was undoubtedly basically to meet the position where, despite the genuine efforts of the players, continuation of play on a fair basis was impossible. In their own interests players should endeavour to play the game on the basis that they attempt to avoid interference and crowding as if Rule 17 did not exist, and should themselves genuinely try to play the ball on all occasions. This attitude would result in: (i) the incoming player standing well clear of the striker while he is playing his shot, thus giving the striker his rightful freedom and himself a better view of the ball and a quicker path to it than if he stood close, and (ii) the striker moving quickly back to the centre of the court after playing the ball and thus being well positioned for the next shot and allowing his opponent a free path to the ball. It is as simple as that, and yet so many players make the match and rules difficult by trying to gain a penalty point through a collision they could have avoided.

Squash can not be played satisfactorily if a player refuses, even though he may have time, to move a little to hit the ball because he thinks that if he stays where he is he can safely appeal for a let—and possibly get a penalty point. A refusal by the referee early in the match to grant such an appeal will soon put things in the right perspective, but he must find justification under the rules to do so.

Players who seek to create a position calling for a let instead of making some effort to avoid one should not be rewarded. In particular, if interference is caused by the incoming striker unnecessarily crowding his opponent immediately after the latter has made his stroke and thereby making it impossible for his opponent to comply with Rule 17, play, in my opinion, should be allowed to continue with no let or penalty point being awarded to the incoming striker because he was not genuinely attempting to get to or play the ball.

Rule 17 is designed to protect the interests of the incoming striker. To avoid penalty, the other player must recover quickly after hitting the ball if it is going to return anywhere on his side of the court. Crossing the ball's line of flight to gain position after striking does not necessarily call for a let or penalty point. The test is whether or not the player gave the incoming striker a fair view of the ball and adequate room to hit it to the front wall or the side wall near the front wall.

The player should position himself to allow his opponent to hit the ball to any part of the front wall or the side wall near the front wall. If a player has not made every effort to do this and is quite obviously covering, say, one-third of the front wall, the referee should stop the game without an appeal and award a penalty point against the transgressor. This is too rarely done and players become used to playing to whatever part of the front wall is available. The referee could take the same course if the opponent covers a corner shot to the front wall or the side wall near the front wall, but this should be on appeal and in many cases a let may be the appropriate verdict as it is difficult for a player or a referee to judge such a marginal case.

Rule 17(d) is often very poorly interpreted, with a penalty point being granted almost automatically against a player whose shot "jaws" from one of the front corners when his opponent is behind him. Ironically the worst jawed shot—the one which comes back across the front of the player who has hit the ball—can seldom make it possible for the latter to be hit in front of the front wall and generally not even a let should be allowed, but in many such cases a penalty is still given.

I well remember all national teams encountering such troubles in the World Championships in New Zealand in 1971 and I spoke strongly about it at a combined teams' meeting. At my suggestion Geoff Hunt, on hitting a jawed ball high up in his next match, crouched down low to give his opponent a clear hit to the front wall and to be ready to chase it — and still had a penalty point awarded against him. I cite this only as a case among many to urge care in making decisions under 17(d).

Many players in championship class have experienced such a variety of interpretations of Rule 17 that they have come to adopt the attitude that the single most important factor in its interpretation in a championship series is absolute consistency. Once they know how the referee stands, they adapt themselves accordingly—and with penalty points becoming more and more prevalent, unfortunate incidents are minimised.

However, this does not get to the crux of the problem—the basic fairness of rulings. As currently active players and perhaps the administrators of the future you should start by studying and discussing the rules and qualifying as referees. You will then understand the basic conception of the rules, particularly Rule 17, and appreciate their overall purpose and soundness. You will also, after long experience, be in a position to put forward recommendations for improvements which you consider would give greater fairness to all players.

I believe two areas need further consideration:

1. The true test of a rule is its application in close, tough competition. In Rule 17 the incoming striker has, quite rightly, full protection and his opponent must make every effort to avoid interfering with him. However, in intense competition many incoming strikers use this protection to create positions which can lead to lets or even penalties in their favour. This enables a player to break up the continuity of attack and pressure which otherwise may be placed on him by his opponent. This outlook should be clearly discouraged and the presence in the rules of a clear direction to referees would ensure that all players play the ball rather than the man. Too much responsibility is presently placed on the referee without clear direction. I suggest that the rules put the onus on each

player, if it is possible and not unfair to him, to take up a position designed to avoid interference when he moves in to take his turn as striker. Such a requirement would create a mental outlook among players which would minimise interference and doubtful refereeing decisions.

2. It has always been a much commented on feature of squash that if you hit your opponent with a ball which would hit the front wall directly you automatically (with a minor exception) win the point. A more recent development is that such a point can be won if the referee decides you could have hit him in this way. The reason for this rule is to make players do everything possible to give their opponents freedom to hit the ball to the front wall, but what a feast of penalty points has resulted no matter if the offending player tries to get out of the way or not! The basic reason for a penalty point in the rules has historically been failure to make every effort to avoid interference. Surely the time has come for consideration of whether or not the penalty in Rule 14(a) should be reduced to a let if the player is hit in front of the front wall despite making every effort to avoid this position. It seems extremely unfair that a player who dominates a rally can lose it through a referee almost automatically granting a penalty against him on an unlucky jawed ball. Surely the balance of justice is a little awry!

Referees associations are associated with most progressive squash rackets associations and I advise you to either become a member of your local referees association or obtain whatever guidelines it has issued so you can learn to anticipate rulings and reduce the possibility of losing vital points on breaches.

If there is one person whose confidence and goodwill every player needs, it is the referee. No referee would be human if he didn't tend to give the benefit of doubt to a player who knows the rules well, tries his best to play within them, calls "not up" when he knows this is the case, and shows good sportsmanship. A player who adopts a belligerent attitude towards the referee seldom gains competitive points.

Finally, a comment on the ball. Unfortunately the specifications in the Rules regarding the requirements for squash balls (Appendix IV) are unsatisfactory because they relate to a "cold" ball rather than to a ball in play. It seems to me that the Rules should require that the performance of balls used in championship matches should be tested on a machine similar in operation to that which projects golf balls to test flight and distance:

The requisite characteristics of the ball's court performance should, in my opinion, be as for the "Australian" ball, decided on by the SRAA ball committee in 1959:

(a) It is possible to drive it hard and low down the wall or across court to a perfect length if hit correctly. These shots can be hit from deep in the court or well up near the front wall with the result that pressure may be applied with length shots.

(b) Boasts may be hit hard and low from against the side wall near the back wall to stop short near the front wall and not reach the other side wall before the second bounce.

(c) Drop shots can be very effective if executed correctly. If indifferently executed they become weak shots.

(d) The ball comes off the floor faster and bounces a little lower than the "English" ball (of a few years ago).

(e) Most important, the degree of competence of the stroke-making is more adequately reflected in results and a good stroke-maker can attack from any position on the court.

Experience has shown that unless a ball used in championship play complies with the above requirements, pressure is taken out of the game and the effects of good stroke play are minimised. At a time when television coverage can make or break a game, it is becoming increasingly important to rectify this situation to attract financial sponsors.

WORLD CHAMPIONS

MEN

Prior to 1967 for amateur status and 1976 for open status there were no official world championships but the British Men's Amateur and British Men's Open titles were unofficially recognised as world titles.

WOMEN

Prior to 1976, which saw the first official World Open Championship for women, the British Women's Amateur Championship was unofficially recognised as the world title.

Mens Amateur		Mens Open		Women's Championship	
1922	T.O. Jameson	1930	D.G. Butcher (Great Britain)	1921	J. Cave (Great Britain)
1923	T.O. Jameson	1931	D.G. Butcher (Great Britain)	1922	S. Huntsman (Great Britain)
1924	W.D. Macpherson	1932	F.D. Amr Bey	1923	N. Cave (Great Britain
1925	V.A. Cazalet	1933	No competition	1924	J. Cave (Great Britain)
1926	J.E. Palmer-Tomkinson	1934	F.D. Amr Bey	1925	C. Fenwick (Great Britain)
1927	V.A. Cazalet	1935	F.D. Amr Bey	1926	C. Fenwick (Great Britain)
1928	W.D. Macpherson	1936	F.D. Amr Bey	1927	J. Cave (Great Britain)
1929	V.A. Cazalet	1937	F.D. Amr Bey	1928	N. Cave (Great Britain)
1930	V.A. Cazalet	1938	J. Dear (Great Britain)	1929	N. Cave (Great Britain)
1931	F.D. Amr Bey	1939-45	No competition	1930	C. Fenwick (Great Britain)
1932	F.D. Amr Bey	1946	M.A. Karim (Egypt)	1931	S. Noel (Great Britain)
1933	F.D. Amr Bey	1947	M.A. Karim (Egypt)	1932	S. Noel (Great Britain)
1934	C.P. Hamilton	1948	M.A. Karim (Egypt)	1933	S. Noel (Great Britain)
1935	F.D. Amr Bey	1949	M.A. Karim (Egypt)	1934	M.E. Lumb (Great Britain)
1936	F.D. Amr Bey	1950	H. Khan (Pakistan)	1935	M.E. Lumb (Great Britain)
1937	F.D. Amr Bey	1951	H. Khan (Pakistan)	1936	M.E. Lumb (Great Britain)
1938	K.C. Gander-Dower	1952	H. Khan (Pakistan)	1937	M.E. Lumb (Great Britain)
1939-45	No competition	1953	H. Khan (Pakistan)	1938	M.E. Lumb (Great Britain)
1946	N.F. Borrett	1954	H. Khan (Pakistan)	1939-45	No competition
1947	N.F. Borrett	1955	H. Khan (Pakistan)	1946	P.J. Curry (Great Britain)
1948	N.F. Borrett	1956	R. Khan (Pakistan)	1947	P.J. Curry (Great Britain)
1949	N.F. Borrett	1957	H. Khan (Pakistan)	1948	P.J. Curry (Great Britain)
1950	N.F. Borrett	1958	A. Khan (Pakistan)	1949	J.R.M. Morgan (Great Britain)
1951	G. Hildick-Smith (South Africa)	1959	A. Khan (Pakistan)	1950	J.R.M. Morgan (Great Britain)
1952	A. Fairbairn	1960	A. Khan (Pakistan)	1951	J.R.M. Morgan (Great Britain)
1953	A. Fairbairn	1961	A. Khan (Pakistan)	1952	J.R.M. Morgan (Great Britain)
1954	R.B.R. Wilson	1962	M. Khan (Pakistan)	1953	J.R.M. Morgan (Great Britain)
1955	I. Amin (Egypt)	1963	A.F.A. Taleb (United Arab Republic)	1954	J.R.M. Morgan (Great Britain)
1956	R.B.R. Wilson (Great Britain)	1964	A.F.A. Taleb (United Arab Republic)	1955	J.R.M. Morgan (Great Britain)
1957	N.H.R.A. Broomfield (Great Britain)	1965	A.F.A. Taleb (United Arab Republic)	1956	J.R.M. Morgan (Great Britain)
1958	N.H.R.A. Broomfield (Great Britain)	1966	J.P. Barrington (Ireland)	1957	J.R.M. Morgan (Great Britain)
1959	I. Amin (Egypt)	1967	J.P. Barrington (Ireland)	1958	J.R.M. Morgan (Great Britain)
1960	M.A. Oddy (Great Britain)	1968	G.B. Hunt (Australia)	1959	H. Macintosh (Great Britain)
1961	M.A. Oddy (Great Britain)	1969	J.P. Barrington (Ireland)	1960	F. Marshall (Great Britain)
1962	K. Hiscoe (Australia)	1970	J.P. Barrington (Ireland)	1961	H. Blundell (Australia)
1963	A.A. Jawaid (Pakistan)	1971	J.P. Barrington (Ireland)	1962	H. Blundell (Australia)
1964	A.A. Jawaid (Pakistan)	1972	J.P. Barrington (Ireland)	1963	H. Blundell (Australia)
1965	A.A. Jawaid (Pakistan)	1973	J.P. Barrington (Ireland)	1964	H. Blundell (Australia)
1966	J.P. Barrington (Ireland)	1974	G.B. Hunt (Australia)	1965	H. McKay (née Blundell (Aust)
1967	G. Hunt (Australia)	1975	Q. Zaman	1966	H. McKay (Australia)
1968	No competition	1976	G.B. Hunt (Australia)	1967	H. McKay (Australia)
1969	G. Hunt (Australia)	1977	G.B. Hunt (Australia)	1968	H. McKay (Australia)
1970	No competition	1979	G.B. Hunt (Australia)	1969	H. McKay (Australia)
1971	G. Hunt (Australia)	1981	Jahangir Khan (Pakistan)	1970	H. McKay (Australia)
1972	No competition			1971	H. McKay (Australia)
1973	C. Nancarrow (Australia)			1972	H. McKay (Australia)
1974	No competition			1973	H. McKay (Australia)
1975	K. Shawcross (Australia)			1974	H. McKay (Australia)
1976	No competition			1975	H. McKay (Australia)
1977	M. Ahmed (Pakistan)			1976	H. McKay (Australia)
1979	Jahangir Khan (Pakistan)			1977	H. McKay (Australia)
1981	Steve Bowditch (Australia)			1979	H. McKay (Australia)
				1981	R. Thorne (Australia)